MOD MEX

MOD MEX
Cooking Vibrant Fiesta Flavors at Home

Scott Linquist
and Joanna Pruess

Photography by Shimon and Tammar Rothstein

Andrews McMeel
Publishing, LLC
Kansas City

07 08 09 10 11 WKT 10 9 8 7 6 5 4 3 2 1

ISBN-13: 978-0-7407-6865-1
ISBN-10: 0-7407-6865-4

Library of Congress Control Number: 2007926843

Food stylist: Brian Preston-Campbell
Prop stylist: Philip Shubin
Photo assistant: Lesley Van Stelten

Photos courtesy of Scott Linquist: 55, 90, 103, 125

www.andrewsmcmeel.com

THIS BOOK IS DEDICATED to my family and friends, who have been too frequently neglected while I pursued a career that has been my complete focus for the past fifteen years. Topping the list is my wonderful wife, **Carrie Sumner**, who brings joy and balance to even the most stressful days. My mother, **Janet Stocks**, believed in me enough to help me through culinary school, and my father, **Ralph Linquist**, was the creative cook of my childhood. My sister, **Michelle Moreno**, helped me even when times were tough. My aunt **Linda Cady** has always been supportive. Finally, this book is also in loving memory of my uncle **Terry Cady**, who I wish could be here to sip a bourbon and share some Mod Mex cuisine.

I also thank my friends **Mike Greco**, **John** and **Gail Onodera**, **Greg** and **Lisa Crosmer**, **Ivy Stark**, **Sean Ryan**, **Ron Soderblom**, and **Edward McMannus**, who are always up for a good party, even if it is only once every couple of years.

CONTENTS

ACKNOWLEDGMENTS

Thank you to the **B.R. Guest** organization, which made all of this possible, especially **Stephen Hanson**, who has been a great leader and inspiration. Thanks to **Michael Jacobs, Donna Rodriguez**, and **Cheryl Perl**, and my bosses **Chris Giarraputo** and **Brett Reichler**, who always keep me on the right track, whether I like it or not. Thank you to our fantastic director of operations and my front-of-the-house teammate **Wendy Schlazer**, and all my fellow corporate chefs and directors of operations: **Shawn Edelman, Paul Sale, Elizabeth Katz, Luis Nieto, Pamela Freidl, Lana Trevison**, and **Anna Marie McCullagh**. Also, to **Janet Hoffman** and **Grace Andrews**, who have taken us in a great new direction over the past year. And to the chefs, managers, and staff from all of our restaurants in this great company: thank you.

In the restaurants' kitchens, I couldn't do what I do without the Dos Caminos team: **Manuel Treviño III**, executive chef; **Roberto Hernandez**, executive chef; and **Hugo Reyes**, executive pastry chef. Our sous chefs: **Carmelo Calixto, Alejandro Sanchez, Stacy Casanova, Tim Krause, David Chiavaroli, Agustin Castro, Jaime Caamano, Luis Ortega, Paul Gaytan**, and the newest additions to the team, **Robert Herrera** and **Michael Radzio**. The leaders of my prep and sauce crew: **Hazael Ortega** and **Miguel Roman**.

Also a great big thanks to all the managers, the entire dining room team, and all the people who make the kitchen run smoothly every day, including our cooks, dishwashers, receivers, and porters. To all of them, I owe a debt of gratitude for their tireless efforts over the past five years.

**PICTURED,
LEFT TO RIGHT:**
Jamie Caamano
Alejandro Sanchez

Tim Krause
David Chiavaroli
Stacy Casanova

Manuel Treviño III
Scott Linquist
Roberto Hernandez

Hugo Reyes
Paul Gaytan

Agustin Castro

A huge thank-you to my coauthor and wonderful collaborator **Joanna Pruess**. Without your tireless effort and dedication to this project, not to mention having to act as my "personal trainer" to get me moving, I would have never been able to complete this book. I am very proud of our accomplishment!

Thank you to our agent, **Jane Dystel**, and our publisher, **Andrews McMeel**, with special thanks to **Kirsty Melville** for your huge enthusiasm for this project. To our superb editors, **Jean Lucas** and **Ann Treistman**, and to **Tim Lynch** for his creative art direction: It was a pleasure working with you. I am also grateful to **Brant Stead** and **Blythe Zava** for your conscientious recipe testing; to **Pamela Harding** for reading the manuscript and offering wise suggestions; to **Eben Klemm**, our corporate manager for wine and spirits, for some of the beverage recipes; and to **Manuel Treviño III** (again) for making sure we used the correct Mexican terminology.

To **Tammar** and **Shimon Rothstein** for your enticing pictures. Your artistic talent and incredible eye perfectly captured the concept of this book!

Finally, thanks to the professionals who helped me to become the chef I am today. **Mary Sue Milliken** and **Susan Feniger** for their inspiration and helping to immerse me in the beauty of cooking Mexican food; **Nancy Oakes** taught me to embrace the wonderful bounty of ingredients available to chefs today; **Alfred Portale**: Your artistry is awe-inspiring; and former Dos Caminos chef **Ivy Stark**, who is one of my best friends and who collaborated on many of the recipes in this book.

INTRODUCTION

After many years of classical culinary training in the restaurants of New York, Los Angeles, and San Francisco, as well as at the Culinary Institute of America (CIA), I have returned to my Mexican roots. You may wonder about my use of "roots," since I'm Swedish in ancestry, my family originally settled in Keokuk, Iowa, and I was born in Southern California. Well, it began in my childhood.

From a very young age, my best friend was Danny Rodriquez. He and his mom, Tina, along with many Hispanic friends who lived near us in Covina, California, helped immerse me in Mexican food and culture. I remember making tacos with Tina's homemade taco shells and salsas and mashing refried beans that weren't from a can.

There were also frequent journeys to Mexico, including family jaunts to Tijuana for *gorditas* (warm, thick *masa* tortillas filled with meat and the most delicious refried beans). By age five, I already had a taste for exotic foods and willingly ate my first escargot there. On a Boy Scout campout in Ensenada in Baja California, I discovered fish tacos sold from a cart and the intense sweetness of ripe fresh mango on a stick, eaten like a Popsicle. Much later, my buddies and I drove down the coast of Baja to surf, eat ceviches and some of the freshest fish imaginable, and participate in some fiery chile-eating contests.

But even with these wonderful memories of eating and preparing Mexican food, when I graduated from the CIA, my main culinary focus was the more prestigious fine-dining cuisines. By a fluke, I ended up at the Border Grill in Santa Monica, California, for my externship, where chef-owners Mary Sue Milliken and Susan Feniger helped me realize my affinity for this beautiful cuisine. They were my mentors, and working as a chef at their restaurant ultimately inspired many of the recipes in this book.

I wasn't quite ready to throw away my aspirations to be the next Alfred Portale or Daniel Boulud, who remain two of my heroes. But, after years of studying the classics, I realized my calling was to prepare what I came to think of as modern Mexican—or "Mod Mex"—cuisine. These dishes, while respectfully based on the age-old traditions of Mexican *mamacitas* and fine cooks from across that diverse country, are adapted to appeal to a generation of food-savvy diners.

Today, people are knowledgeable about cooking and want foods with bold flavors and vibrant colors that are prepared with the finest, healthiest ingredients available. They are also looking for authenticity in their restaurant experiences. At Dos Caminos, I have found the perfect venue to showcase my approach to modern Mexican cooking, including the *fiesta* (party) environment.

Mexican food is very approachable. Everyone loves guacamole and margaritas made with Mexico's most famous export, tequila. Fresh and bottled salsas—from mild to fiery hot—are about to replace ketchup as this country's favorite condiment at home and in restaurants. To build on these experiences, I encourage my guests and readers of this book to try *bocaditos* ("little bites") such as tacos, tamales, and ceviches; delicious *mole* sauces; and seductive desserts, like my favorite, *Crepas de Cajeta* (Roasted Banana Crepes) with *dulce de leche*, a creamy goat's milk caramel sauce.

Over the past fifteen years, I've continued to refine my menus and I've taken groups of food professionals to Mexico repeatedly to study the culture and cuisine. I've gone home to Puebla with some of my chefs, I've eaten *barbacoa* under a thatched-roof *palapa* with an outdoor kitchen that is now a tourist destination in Oaxaca, and I have spent countless days and weeks cooking with great and humble cooks from Mexico City to the Yucatán.

My cooking reflects these experiences and the enormous diversity of regional specialties throughout the country. Many dishes are updated traditional preparations. Others are originals inspired by Mexican techniques and ingredients that I combine with my classic culinary training.

Home cooks are similarly looking for flavorful, exciting recipes to spice up the meals they prepare. In this book, my wonderful collaborator, Joanna Pruess, has kept the heart and soul of the dishes we serve in the restaurant, while making them straightforward and easy to follow at home. Mexican ingredients are now readily available at local supermarkets, ethnic grocery stores, or gourmet stores. For more obscure items and special cooking utensils, the Internet is a very useful resource. I also suggest alternatives for ingredients that may be difficult to find.

Traditionalists may assert that certain dishes like *moles* must be made as they always have been, but I believe in an innovative, forward-thinking frame of mind. Over time, I have learned that respectful change can result in more approachable, fresher dishes that are often more appealing to contemporary diners. To me, this is "Mod Mex."

¡BUEN PROVECHO!

MEXICAN ESSENTIALS

Chapter One: BASIC TECHNIQUES AND COOKING EQUIPMENT

SALSAS

In Mexico, the word "salsa" means any sauce, whereas in the United States, it refers to what Mexicans call a "table salsa." Most Mexican meals would not be complete without a salsa or two or even more. These days, we can't seem to get enough of these zesty, chunky or smooth sauces and have taken to using them not only with tortilla chips but also on grilled chicken breasts, steaks, baked or fried potatoes, and even salads.

In Mexican cooking, there are hundreds of salsas, each with many potential variations. Some are *cruda*, or raw; others are cooked in a variety of ways, such as boiled (the most common method), roasted in an oven, charred under a broiler, or grilled on a barbecue to add a smokier, more full-bodied flavor. Each results in significantly different salsas. Using different chiles also intensifies the heat and can dramatically alter the flavor. Salsas can be diced and chunky or a smooth purée.

Generally, red salsas are made with tomatoes as the base, whereas a green sauce, salsa verde, starts with tomatillos. Other ingredients typically include onions, chile peppers, garlic, and herbs, and usually a touch of lime juice. Most tomato salsas are prepared with jalapeño or serrano chiles or, to really fire it up, fresh habaneros. But using dried chiles, like smoky chipotles or spicy arbol chiles, also adds a unique flavor. Combining fresh and dried chiles is yet another option.

Also you can use different herbs, including cilantro (the most frequently used), oregano, and epazote, which tastes like a cross between mint, basil, and oregano.

Beyond the chunky, often uncooked salsas that are most familiar to us, you will discover several others that are simple and made fresh to serve as a condiment to complement almost any dish in this book. I recommend making salsas in batches, keeping them in the refrigerator, and using them regularly to enhance even the simplest piece of grilled fish or steak.

In Mexico as well as in the United States, we also garnish foods with bottled hot sauces—such as Tabasco and my personal favorite, Valentina—which are almost like super-condensed essence of spicy salsa.

BASIC PICO DE GALLO

Pico de gallo is probably the best-known uncooked tomato salsa. The name means "rooster's beak" in Spanish, and it's a fresher, less "saucy" take on salsa. It's typically used as the partner for tortilla chips. I include variations on basic pico de gallo throughout this book.

6 plum tomatoes, seeded and cut into small cubes
1 medium red onion, chopped
1 to 3 serrano or jalapeño chiles, chopped
¼ cup chopped fresh cilantro leaves
1 tablespoon fresh lime juice
Kosher salt

Makes 2 cups

Mix all of the ingredients together, season with about ½ teaspoon of salt or to taste, and refrigerate for 1 hour.

BASIC TOMATO SALSA

You can boil, roast, or grill the tomatoes in this basic salsa or use them raw. If you use them raw, the salsa will be a thinner consistency. For this and the following salsa, the method is the same.

Makes 2½ cups

Toast and rehydrate the chiles (see page 6). If you choose to cook the tomatoes, onion, and garlic, roast them in a 400°F oven for 15 to 30 minutes, until lightly browned and soft; grill them until charred; or boil them until tender. Otherwise, use them uncooked. Combine the vegetables in the jar of an electric blender with the chiles, cilantro, vinegar, salt, and pepper, and purée until the desired consistency, either chunky-smooth or completely smooth. Store covered in the refrigerator in a nonreactive container for up to a week.

4 arbol chiles

6 plum tomatoes

1 medium yellow onion, quartered

2 cloves garlic

½ cup loosely packed fresh cilantro leaves

2 tablespoons red wine or apple cider vinegar

Kosher salt and freshly ground black pepper

BASIC SALSA VERDE

This version uses tomatillos to create salsa verde, or green salsa.

Makes 2 cups

Follow the directions for Basic Tomato Salsa.

6 large tomatillos, husked

1 medium yellow onion, quartered

2 cloves garlic

1 to 3 jalapeño or serrano chiles, stemmed and seeded

½ cup loosely packed fresh cilantro leaves

2 tablespoons freshly squeezed lime juice

Kosher salt and freshly ground black pepper

GUACAMOLE

For great guacamole, use a lava-stone *molcajete* (see page 10), and prepare the guacamole just before eating. (Even if you don't have a *molcajete,* you can make a good guacamole at home, using a bowl and the back of a spoon.) Use the freshest possible ingredients and pound them all together into a chunky-smooth texture.

BASIC GUACAMOLE

California-grown Haas avocados have a creamier, denser texture than all other varieties. Serve this dip with warm tortilla chips, or use it as a spread in other recipes. You can adjust the spice level up or down by changing the amount of chiles you add. This recipe doubles well for a crowd.

Serves 4

Mash together 1 tablespoon of the cilantro, 1 teaspoon of the onion, 1 teaspoon of the chile, and ½ teaspoon of salt in the bottom of a *molcajete* or medium-size bowl.

Add the avocados and gently mash with a fork until chunky-smooth. Fold the remaining cilantro, onion, and chile into the mixture. Stir in the tomato and lime juice, adjust the seasonings to taste, and serve with a basket of warm corn tortilla chips.

2 tablespoons finely chopped fresh cilantro leaves

2 teaspoons finely chopped yellow onion

2 teaspoons minced jalapeño or serrano chiles, seeds and membranes removed, if desired

Kosher or coarse salt

2 large ripe avocados, peeled and seeded

2 tablespoons cored, seeded, and finely chopped plum tomato (1 small tomato)

2 teaspoons freshly squeezed lime juice

Warm tortilla chips, for serving

DRESSING UP GUACAMOLE

The basic guacamole recipe can be varied easily by gently folding a few of the following extra ingredients into the mixture before serving:

LOBSTER GUACAMOLE

Meat from 1 (1-pound) lobster, steamed, cooled, and coarsely chopped, or 4 ounces cooked lobster meat

Japanese pickled ginger, for garnish

MANGO GUACAMOLE

1 large ripe mango, peeled, seeded, and diced (Any fruit, such as fresh berries, seedless grapes, or papaya will also work.)

CHIPOTLE–GOAT CHEESE GUACAMOLE

4 ounces goat cheese, crumbled (about ½ cup)

2 tablespoons chopped canned chipotle chiles

ARTICHOKE GUACAMOLE WITH TOASTED PINE NUTS

1 cup chopped marinated artichoke hearts

¼ cup toasted pine nuts

CHILES

Chiles are an essential flavoring in countless Mexican dishes, including the Chocolate Layer Cake with Morita Chile Mousse and Pistachio *Palanquetta* on page 162. They vary widely in taste and heat; to learn more specific details about the various chiles used in these recipes, please refer to the Glossary. Although supermarkets have expanded their selection of fresh and dried chile peppers, unless you live in a neighborhood with a sizable Hispanic population, you may have to look in smaller ethnic grocery stores or go online to find some of the more obscure varieties (see Sources). The number of sources for these ingredients is expanding quite rapidly with our increased appreciation for them.

Generally, the smaller the top of the chile, where it attaches to the stem, the hotter it is. The hottest parts of any chile are the membranes inside, next to the seeds. If you prefer somewhat milder flavors, remove the membranes and the seeds from a chile before using it in a recipe.

TO PREPARE CHILES AND OTHER PEPPERS

Working with chile peppers can cause you to weep in pain! If you are not careful, the oil in the peppers can get on your hands, under your nails, or on just about any area the oil comes in contact with, and you can spread it very easily by touching another part of your body. The best advice I have for you is to wear rubber gloves when working with chiles (the thin ones that doctors use are the best), and *don't touch your eyes* for several hours afterward, even if you have washed your hands.

ROASTING: Often fresh chiles are peeled and roasted. Roast the chiles over high heat, directly on a gas burner, over an open flame, or under the broiler until the skin begins to blister and turn black. Use tongs to turn them, as they should to be charred all over, even on the ends. Transfer the chiles to a bowl, cover tightly with plastic wrap until cooled, and then carefully scrape off the skin so that they do not break or split. A paring knife works best for this. Cut a slit from the stem toward the tip and remove the seeds and membranes, if desired.

TOASTING AND REHYDRATING: For dried chiles, pull off the stems and pull out the seeds. Cook the chiles in a hot, dry skillet until the skins blister slightly and you smell a toasty aroma. Let the chiles cool, and then rehydrate them: In a small saucepan, cover the toasted dried chiles with water, bring just to a boil, remove the pan from the heat, and let them cool in the liquid for 5 to 10 minutes. If needed in puréed form, use tongs or a slotted spoon to transfer the chiles to the jar of an electric blender and purée, adding as little of the soaking liquid as necessary to make a smooth paste.

HOW HOT IS THAT CHILE PEPPER?

The heat level of different chile peppers is measured on a scale devised by Wilbur Scoville, a chemist who worked for the Parke-Davis Pharmaceutical Company, in 1912. Starting from sweet bell peppers with no heat units, they go to fiery habaneros, which are close to pure capsaicin (pepper).

PEPPER TYPE	HEAT RATING (IN SCOVILLE HEAT UNITS*)
Habanero	100,000–300,000
Pequin	75,000
Cayenne	30,000–40,000
Arbol	25,000
Smoked jalapeño (chipotle)	10,000–15,000
Serrano	7,000–25,000
Guajillo	5,000
Jalapeño (green)	2,500–5,000
Poblano	2,500–3,000
Pasilla	2,500
Ancho	1,000–2,000
New Mexican	500–1,000
Bell	0–100

MILD: 0–5,000

MEDIUM: 5,000–20,000

HOT: 20,000–70,000

EXTREMELY HOT: 70,000–300,000

* First created in 1912, the Scoville heat unit is the closest thing to a standard measure for the heat of a pepper. The number of units is determined by adding sugar to a solution until the taste of the pepper can no longer be detected. The more sugar required, the higher the level of spice and thus a higher number of Scoville units.

ROASTING VEGETABLES AND GARLIC FOR SAUCES

Put garlic, tomatoes, onions, and other vegetables on an oiled sheet pan. Roast them in a preheated 400°F oven until the skins of the tomatoes are blistered and the onions are lightly browned and soft, 15 to 30 minutes, depending on your stove and the desired degree of doneness. Remove, cool, and continue with recipe.

MASA

Masa is the Spanish word for the corn dough used to make tortillas, tamales, and other Mexican dishes. In traditional Mexican cooking, *masa* is made by soaking corn in warm water and powdered limestone and then grinding it into a paste. Fortunately, today we can buy *masa harina*, a corn flower used for dough. You can find it in stores that sell Mexican products. "Maseca" is the most common brand of corn flour. Maseca offers finely ground corn flour for making tortillas and other dishes like *sopes*, as well as coarsely ground corn flour especially milled for tamales, which gives these dishes their characteristic toothsome texture.

Although the use of the word *masa* and *masa harina* for both dough and flour can be confusing, there is no uncertainty about the role that tortillas, made with finely ground corn flour, play in Mexican cooking. No meal would be complete without a big basket of them, nicely warmed.

To make fresh tortillas, Mexicans use a tortilla press, called a *prensa de tortilla* (see page 10). Another option is to press the dough between two books covered with plastic wrap. In Mexico, you also see women using their hands to pat the dough into flat tortillas.

BASIC DOUGH (MASA) FOR TORTILLAS, EMPANADAS, AND SOPES

This will make a large quantity of tortilla products. You can cut the recipe in half or wrap any remaining dough in plastic and refrigerate it for up to 5 days.

Makes 8 cups

5 cups finely ground corn flour for tortillas
3 cups warm water
1 tablespoon kosher salt

Mix the corn flour with the water and salt in the bowl of a stand mixer using the paddle attachment on medium speed until it is evenly distributed and forms a cohesive, not sticky, semifirm dough when pressed together. To mix by hand, combine ingredients in a bowl with a fork. Gather into a ball and knead dough until smooth and no longer sticky. Cover the dough with plastic wrap and refrigerate for ½ hour or up to 5 days. Typically, a 1½-tablespoon ball of dough is used to make a 4-inch tortilla.

Place the dough on a *prensa* lined with plastic wrap and press the dough into a flat disk, or press it between two books covered with plastic wrap. Cook on a hot griddle for 2 to 3 minutes per side. Tortillas are best when prepared fresh and served right off the griddle.

CREMA

Deliciously thick, slightly tangy crema is used like sour cream or crème fraîche in many Mexican dishes. It is also sometimes sweetened, as for Banana Pancakes with *Piloncillo* Syrup and Spiced Crema (page 171). Once made, it can be kept, refrigerated, for up to one week.

BASIC CREMA

2 cups heavy cream
¼ cup buttermilk

Makes 2¼ cups

In a small saucepan, heat the cream to about 90°F. Pour the cream into a bowl, whisk in the buttermilk, and cover with cheesecloth or a dry, clean towel. Set in a warm place, such as a gas oven with just the pilot light on, overnight until thickened. If still not thickened, leave for 2 to 4 hours more. Stir well, cover, and refrigerate

USEFUL EQUIPMENT

You can make all of the dishes in this book with the equipment probably already in your kitchen. However, for a more authentic experience, here are a few uniquely Mexican cooking tools to try:

CAZUELA: A large, shallow pottery or cast-iron dish, about 2 inches deep, with a glazed interior and two handles, used for slowly simmering stewlike casseroles. The exteriors of *cazuelas* are sometimes painted in vibrant colors.

COMAL: A large round griddle, typically made of aluminum, cast iron, or clay, used to heat tortillas and roast vegetables or chiles. Newer versions have a non-stick finish.

MOLCAJETE: A lava-stone mortar that stands on three legs. It is used with a pestle to grind spices and to pound avocados into chunky-smooth guacamole.

PRENSA DE TORTILLA: A tortilla press is made of cast iron, wood, or aluminum with a base, top, and handle. A small ball of dough is placed between the two large round plates or blocks of wood, which are pressed together to form a tortilla. The plates are lined with plastic wrap to prevent the dough from sticking. As an alternative, you can press the dough between two books covered with plastic wrap.

TUMBADA: A wide, shallow earthenware cooking and serving vessel used to make the Mexican-style paella dish by the same name.

BOCADITOS

Chapter Two: LITTLE BITES
AND STARTERS

I THINK OF BOCADITOS as the finger foods or small bites

that are a way of life in Mexico. Many of the dishes I love were inspired by street snacks and market foods I have eaten during my travels there. Whether they are the tasty fish tacos that I remember from a Boy Scout trip to Ensenada or a great Veracruz-style ceviche that I tasted on the Gulf Coast of Mexico, these foods are often best when you buy them on the street from carts or stands.

For example, what would Mexican food be without the taco stand? *Taquerías* are common throughout Mexico as well as in every Mexican community in the United States. I have also enjoyed them on a dusty trail in Valle de Guadalupe (Baja wine country) and in the Hotel Camino Real, a former convent in downtown Oaxaca. At that very spiritual oasis, the brilliant platters of *bocaditos* include a combination of quesadillas, taquitos, empanadas, and Oaxaca's most famous munchy, *chapulines*—crispy spiced grasshoppers—which I love to eat in a warm tortilla with guacamole. (If that isn't your cup of tea, don't worry. There are no recipes for crispy insects in this book.)

Be creative with your *bocaditos*. Mix and match them to suit the occasion. These bold and spicy flavors go well with cocktails and are great for parties. Their tremendous versatility makes them perfect to platter up for guests as appetizers for New Year's Eve, Cinco de Mayo, or Super Bowl Sunday celebrations, or as an appetizer or main course for a family meal.

Above all, *bocaditos* are meant to be fun foods with zippy flavors that wake up your taste buds and fiery chiles that give you a natural high. In this chapter, I have translated the spirit of these fresh-tasting little bites for meals at home. To me, *bocaditos* are among the most exciting Mexican foods, and I have a real fondness for them in my heart.

PORK CARNITAS TACOS WITH SERRANO CHILE SALSA

Carnitas are cubes of pork that are slowly braised in fat, like confit of duck, until they are meltingly tender. This version uses Coca-Cola, which is beloved in Mexico. Cola drinks are great tenderizers and add a distinctive caramel-like sweetness that nicely accents the pork. Lard is definitely the preferred fat for this recipe because of the flavor it imparts.

Serves 6 (12 tacos)

Preheat the oven to 300°F.

In a large casserole or Dutch oven, melt the lard or heat the oil over medium heat. Stir in the pork, orange juice, Coca-Cola, condensed milk, peppercorns, bay leaves, garlic, cinnamon, and salt. Transfer the pot to the oven and cook for 2 to 2½ hours, until the meat is very tender and shreds easily. Remove the pot from the oven. Transfer the meat from the pot to a flat dish or bowl using a slotted spoon to drain the liquid. Let stand until it is cool enough to handle, and then cut it into small cubes or shred by hand.

Divide the *carnitas* evenly among 12 warm tortillas. Fold each tortilla in half, and serve 2 per person with your favorite salsa.

3 pounds lard (see Glossary), or 6 cups canola oil

1½ pounds boneless pork butt, trimmed and cut into 2 by 2-inch cubes

½ cup freshly squeezed orange juice

½ cup Coca-Cola or other cola drink

¼ cup canned sweetened condensed milk

5 whole black peppercorns

2 bay leaves

2 cloves garlic, smashed

1 stick cinnamon, preferably Mexican

½ tablespoon kosher salt

12 (6-inch) corn tortillas, purchased or homemade (page 9)

Salsa of choice (see page 2), for serving

LARD—NOT NECESSARILY A DIETARY NO-NO

While lard has been relatively out of favor in the United States, recent studies show that it has less saturated fat than butter and more of the monounsaturated fats that are good for you.

TACOS AL PASTOR WITH ROASTED PINEAPPLE PICO DE GALLO

When I was in Puebla, locals told me that the *al pastor,* or "shepherd"-style, marinade originated there. But—as commonly happens with food in Mexico—others argue that the marinade is from Mexico City. These tacos are also known as *tacos arabes,* or Arab-style tacos, because of the filling's similarity to Lebanese spit-roasted meat. Traditionally, layers of pork are marinated in a secret recipe that varies from vendor to vendor and then skewered on an upright spit with fresh pineapple and onion. If you don't own a rotisserie, you can either grill or broil the meat. The marinade can also be brushed on pork chops, grilled chicken breasts, or even on a steak or a piece of fish.

AL PASTOR MARINADE

3 ancho chiles

3 guajillo chiles

4 cloves garlic

4 bay leaves

1 medium yellow onion, quartered

2 tablespoons achiote paste (see Glossary)

2 tablespoons kosher salt

1 teaspoon ground cumin

1 teaspoon dried oregano, preferably
   Mexican

1 teaspoon freshly ground black pepper

1 teaspoon fresh thyme leaves, chopped

½ teaspoon ground allspice

½ teaspoon ground cinnamon

½ teaspoon ground cloves

2 cups water

½ cup apple cider vinegar or red or white
   wine vinegar

3 pounds boneless pork butt, thinly sliced

Kosher salt

continued on next page

Serves 12 (24 tacos)

MAKE THE MARINADE: Toast and rehydrate the chiles (see page 6). Using a slotted spoon, transfer the chiles to the jar of an electric blender along with all of the remaining marinade ingredients and purée until smooth. Set aside.

Put the pork slices between two sheets of waxed paper or plastic wrap and, using a meat pounder or the back of a heavy pan, flatten into ½-inch-thick slices. Season with salt, put in a large nonreactive mixing bowl, and pour in about 2 cups of the marinade, turning to coat evenly. Cover the bowl and refrigerate for at least 8 hours or overnight. The remaining marinade may be kept in a tightly covered container in the refrigerator for up to 1 week or frozen for up to 3 months.

Preheat a rotisserie. Lift the pork from the marinade. Slide the whole onion (for the pico de gallo) onto the skewer, thread the meat slices onto the skewer, and then add the pineapple slices (for the pico de gallo). Put the skewer on the rotisserie to cook.

TACOS

North of the border, we tend to think of tacos as shaped crispy corn tortilla shells that are filled and sometimes warmed before serving. In Mexico, tacos are warm, soft corn tortillas that are simply filled and folded in half before being eaten.

As the meat browns on the outside, use a sharp knife to slice off paper-thin layers of meat. Repeat this process until all of the meat has been cooked and sliced.

If you do not have a rotisserie, slice the onion and pineapple and put the slices along with the pork on a grill or under the broiler and cook until the meat is cooked medium-well, 3 to 4 minutes on each side, turning once. (The onion and pineapple will be heated and marked with grill marks.)

MAKE THE PICO DE GALLO: Remove the roasted onion and pineapple from the skewer and chop into ½-inch cubes. Toss them with the cilantro, serrano chiles, and lime juice, and season to taste with salt. Fill each tortilla with 1 to 2 heaping tablespoons of meat and top with a spoonful of pico de gallo.

ROASTED PINEAPPLE PICO DE GALLO

1 whole medium yellow onion, peeled

¼ fresh pineapple, peeled and cut crosswise but not cored

½ cup chopped fresh cilantro leaves

¼ cup thinly sliced serrano chiles

2 tablespoons freshly squeezed lime juice

Kosher salt

24 (6-inch) corn tortillas, purchased or homemade (page 9)

GRILLED CHICKEN TACOS AL CARBÓN
WITH FRESH ORANGE SALSITA

The name *al carbón* means "cooking over coals" and refers to the charred surface of the meat derived from the grilling process. This simple recipe is perfect for a summer barbecue.

Serves 6 (12 tacos)

In a small bowl, blend the orange juice, achiote paste, honey, and salt. Put the chicken breasts into a large bowl, pour on the achiote marinade, and turn to coat evenly. Cover and refrigerate for at least 2 hours or up to a day in advance of grilling.

MAKE THE SALSITA: Combine all of the salsita ingredients in a medium-size bowl, toss gently, and refrigerate until ready to serve. The salsita can be made up to an hour in advance, but if making it ahead of time, add the salt just before serving.

Heat a barbecue until hot and brush the grill rack with oil. Lift the chicken breasts from the marinade and discard the marinade. Season on both sides with salt and pepper and grill until nicely charred, 5 to 7 minutes per side, turning once. The internal temperature should be 165°F on an instant-read thermometer. Using tongs, remove the breasts, let rest for 1 to 2 minutes, and then slice crosswise into thin strips. Meanwhile, wrap the tortillas in aluminum foil and heat on the grill for 5 minutes.

To serve, spoon 1 tablespoon of guacamole onto each tortilla, add about ¼ cup of grilled chicken, and top with 2 tablespoons of salsita. Serve warm.

½ cup freshly squeezed orange juice
¼ cup achiote paste (see Glossary)
1 tablespoon honey
½ teaspoon kosher salt
2 pounds boneless, skinless chicken breasts

ORANGE SALSITA

4 Navel or Valencia oranges, peeled and cut into segments
1 red bell pepper, seeds and membranes removed, cut into thin strips
1 yellow bell pepper, seeds and membranes removed, cut into thin strips
1 poblano chile, stemmed, seeded, membranes removed, and cut into thin strips
¼ cup finely chopped fresh cilantro leaves
¼ cup apple cider vinegar
2 tablespoons honey
1 teaspoon kosher salt

Freshly ground black pepper
12 (6-inch) corn tortillas, purchased or homemade (page 9)
2 cups guacamole (page 5)

CUTTING AN ORANGE INTO SEGMENTS

Using a sharp paring knife, cut off the colored peel and white pith from the orange. To remove the sections, cut a narrow slice off the top and bottom of the orange. Working over a strainer, make an incision next to the membrane of one section and another cut on the other side of the section, letting the sections fall into the strainer as they are loosened.

Continue working around the orange. After all the sections have been removed, squeeze the juice from the orange core into a separate bowl and reserve. This technique works for other citrus fruits as well. (It is also possible to slice the orange in half and remove the segments as you would cut a grapefruit, using a grapefruit knife.)

CASCABEL CHILE-MARINATED CARNE ASADA TACOS
WITH CARAMELIZED ONIONS, PICO DE GALLO, AND COTIJA CHEESE

Carne asada usually refers to steak that is pounded flat and then marinated and cooked on a flat griddle or *comal* (see page 10), which sears the outside of the meat. The marinated meat in this traditional recipe tastes fresh and modern, set off by the dry, salty *cotija* cheese. If you don't have a *comal,* cook the meat on a barbecue or on top of the stove in a heavy skillet. Cascabel chiles have a nice, toasty red chile flavor, but they are not too spicy.

MARINADE

6 cascabel chiles

1 arbol chile

½ cup reserved cooking liquid from soaking the chiles

1 small yellow onion, quartered

3 cloves garlic

½ cup apple cider vinegar

¼ cup Maggi sauce or Worcestershire sauce

2 tablespoons freshly squeezed lime juice

½ tablespoon dried oregano, preferably Mexican

1 teaspoon kosher salt

1½ pounds (1-inch-thick) sirloin steak, butterflied (or ask the butcher to do this)

Kosher salt and freshly ground black pepper

12 (6-inch) corn tortillas, purchased or homemade (page 9)

1 cup guacamole (page 5)

2 cups pico de gallo (page 2)

2 ounces cotija or feta cheese, grated (about ½ cup)

Salsa of choice (see page 2)

Serves 6 (12 tacos)

Preheat the oven to 400°F.

MAKE THE MARINADE: Toast and rehydrate the chiles (see page 6). Meanwhile, roast the onion on a baking sheet for 10 to 12 minutes, until brown (see page 7). Combine the chiles and onion with the remaining marinade ingredients in the jar of an electric blender and purée until smooth.

In a large bowl, toss the steak with the marinade, making sure that it is well coated. Cover and refrigerate for 8 hours or overnight.

Heat the barbecue until hot. Lift the meat from the marinade and discard the marinade. Season the steaks on both sides with salt and pepper and grill to the desired degree of doneness, 2 to 3 minutes per side for medium-rare, turning once. Remove to a cutting board, let rest for 1 to 2 minutes, and then slice crosswise into ½-inch-wide strips.

While the steak is cooking, wrap the tortillas in aluminum foil and heat them on the grill for about 5 minutes.

To serve, spoon 1 tablespoon of guacamole onto each warm tortilla. Add about ¼ cup of carne asada, 1 to 2 tablespoons of pico de gallo, and about 1 teaspoon *cotija* cheese. Serve 2 per person with salsa on the side.

BAJA-STYLE MAHI-MAHI TACOS

Baja is famous for its beer-battered fried fish tacos. The tempting contrast of textures and tastes make this a wonderful snack with crunchy cucumber slaw, creamy chipotle *mayonesa*, warm tortillas, and crispy fried fish. For a healthier but equally delicious version of this classic dish, use grilled fish.

Serves 6

MAKE THE RELISH: Combine the cucumbers, tomatoes, red onion, cabbage, cilantro, and chile in a nonreactive bowl. Combine the orange, grapefruit, and lime juices and pour over the vegetables. Add the salt, toss to blend, and set aside for 30 minutes.

MAKE THE BATTER: In a medium-size mixing bowl, combine the flour, chile powder, salt, and baking powder and mix together. In another bowl, whisk the egg until smooth, and then stir in the beer. Whisk the dry ingredients into the liquids, stirring until smooth.

In a large, deep skillet, pour in enough oil to measure 1 inch deep. Heat the oil over high heat until hot, about 350°F on an instant-read thermometer. Dip the pieces of fish into the batter, letting the excess fall back into the bowl, and fry until golden brown, about 4 minutes, turn, and cook the second side for the same amount of time. Remove the fish pieces with a metal spatula or slotted spoon and blot on paper towels to remove excess oil.

Meanwhile, peel, seed, and mash the avocado with a fork in a small bowl. Wrap the tortillas in aluminum foil and quickly warm in the oven, then spread each one with a little avocado. Put 1 piece of fish on each tortilla, spoon on a tablespoon of Citrus-Cucumber Relish and a scant tablespoon of Chipotle Aioli, and fold in half. Serve 2 tacos on each plate with plenty of table salsa.

GRILLED TACOS

Prepare Baja-Style Mahi-Mahi Tacos, but do not make the batter. Preheat a gas or an electric grill, or light the broiler. Position the grill rack about 4 inches from the heat. Grill the mahi-mahi for 4 minutes on each side, turning once, or until just cooked through. Serve with the same garnishes.

CITRUS-CUCUMBER RELISH

3 Kirby or pickling cucumbers, peeled, seeded, and cut into thin strips
3 plum tomatoes, cored and cut into thin strips
1 small red onion, cut in half and sliced into thin strips
1 cup shredded white cabbage
¼ cup chopped fresh cilantro leaves
1 serrano chile, seeded, if desired, and thinly sliced
½ cup freshly squeezed orange juice
2 tablespoons freshly squeezed grapefruit juice
1 tablespoon freshly squeezed lime juice
1 tablespoon kosher salt

BATTER

1½ cups all-purpose flour
1 tablespoon ancho chile powder
1 tablespoon kosher salt
1 teaspoon baking powder
1 large egg
1 (12-ounce) can light Mexican beer, such as Tecate, very cold

Canola oil, for frying
2 pounds mahi-mahi steaks, cut into 4-inch-wide strips
12 (6-inch) corn tortillas, purchased or homemade (page 9)
1 ripe avocado
½ cup Chipotle Aioli, prepared without the scallions and honey (page 55)
Salsa of choice (see page 2)

LOBSTER TACOS
WITH ROASTED TOMATO-CHIPOTLE SALSITA AND JICAMA SLAW

Baja is known for its lobster festivals, and one local specialty is these tacos. Their tangy tomato and spicy chipotle filling is offset by the toothsome crunch of the jicama slaw. The slaw is best made fresh and used immediately. However, if you need to make it in advance, toss all of the ingredients together except the salt, cover and refrigerate it for up to an hour, and add salt just prior to serving. You can substitute shrimp for the lobster in this recipe.

Kosher salt

3 (1-pound) lobsters, or 1½ pounds cooked
   lobster or shrimp

1 tablespoon olive oil

Freshly ground pepper

ROASTED TOMATO-CHIPOTLE SALSITA

3 plum tomatoes, quartered lengthwise

1 tablespoon butter

1 medium-size yellow onion, cut in half and
   sliced into thin strips

2 cloves garlic, thinly sliced

2 canned chipotle chiles in adobo, chopped

¼ cup apple cider vinegar

1½ ounces piloncillo, finely chopped (about
   3 tablespoons), or dark brown sugar

1 teaspoons kosher salt

JICAMA SLAW

2 small Navel or Valencia oranges, peeled
   and cut into segments (see sidebar,
   page 17)

1 serrano chile, sliced very thinly crosswise

½ pound jicama, peeled and cut into thin
   strips

1 small red onion, cut in half lengthwise and
   sliced crosswise into thin strips

¼ cup chopped fresh cilantro leaves

2 tablespoons freshly squeezed orange
   juice

continued on next page

Serves 6 (12 tacos)

If cooking the lobsters, bring at least 4 quarts of salted water to a rolling boil in a large pot. Add the lobsters, cover the pot, return the water to a boil, and cook the lobsters for 7 minutes more, or until the shells are bright red. Remove with tongs, wrap each lobster in a piece of aluminum foil, and let cool. Using a nutcracker or the back of a large knife, crack the shells and remove the meat in large chunks. Put the meat into a bowl, cover, and refrigerate for up to 2 hours.

MAKE THE SALSITA: Preheat the oven to 350°F. Put the tomatoes on a baking sheet and bake until they start to dry and turn brown, about 30 minutes, turning occasionally. Remove and cool on the baking sheet.

Meanwhile, heat a large skillet over medium heat. Add the butter and onion and sauté over medium heat until the onion is lightly brown, about 6 minutes, stirring occasionally. Stir in the garlic and cook for 1 minute longer. Remove from the heat.

In a small saucepan, combine the chipotles, vinegar, *piloncillo*, and salt over low heat and simmer until the sugar has dissolved and the mixture has a syrupy consistency, about 5 minutes. In a large bowl, toss together the roasted tomatoes, caramelized onions, garlic, and chile-vinegar syrup and taste to adjust the seasonings.

CHORIZO, POTATO, AND GOAT CHEESE SOR

Sopes are small, round cornmeal tartlets like thick tortillas with the ⬤
and then cooked on a griddle. They can be made any size, and smalle
d'oeuvres. These *sopes* are made with Mexican chorizo, pork sausag
pepper. Don't confuse the Mexican version with Spanish chorizo, whic
vibrant flavor of the meat is a nice contrast to the creamy goat chees

Makes 12 (2½-inch) *sopes*

MAKE THE FILLING: Heat 1 tablespoon of the oil in a large
skillet over medium-high heat. Add the chorizo and brown
on all sides, turning often. Transfer the chorizo to a bowl
with a slotted spoon and discard all but a tablespoon of
the fat from the pan. Add the onions to the same skillet
and sauté over medium heat until lightly browned, about 5
minutes. Stir in the garlic, cook for 1 minute, and then add
the jalapeño and arbol chiles and oregano and continue to
cook for 5 minutes more.

Heat the remaining 3 tablespoons of oil in a second large
skillet over medium-high heat. Add the potatoes and fry
until brown and cooked through, about 6 to 8 minutes,
turning to color evenly. Remove with a slotted spoon, drain
on paper towels, season with salt and pepper, and then
fold into the chorizo mixture.

Spread each *sope* with 1 teaspoon of goat cheese and 1
teaspoon of Salsa Pasilla, and top with 2 tablespoons of
the chorizo-potato mixture. Garnish each with a tiny dab of
crema on top.

BARBECUED PORK SOPES WITH PICKLED ONIONS

Makes 6 (2½-inch) *sopes*

This *sope* recipe uses a combination of other recipes
in this book. (Mexican leftovers are very handy for
dishes like this!) Hopefully you will have all or part
of this prepared already.

MAKE THE SLAW: Toss all of the ingredients in a large
mixing bowl and season to taste with salt. Set aside. Refrigerate if made more than 1 hour ahead of time.

Preheat a barbecue, gas grill, or broiler. Wrap the tortillas
in aluminum foil and heat them on the grill for 5 minutes.

Toss the lobster meat with the olive oil. Season with salt
and pepper and grill the pieces just long enough to warm
the meat through and char the outside, about 2 minutes on
each side. Remove and cut into bite-size pieces.

In each tortilla, put a slice of avocado, a scant ¼ cup of
lobster meat, and 2 tablespoons of salsita, and garnish
with about 2 tablespoons of slaw. Roll into a cone, fold the
bottom upward to hold the filling inside, and serve with
lime wedges and plenty of table salsa.

2 tablespoons freshly squeezed lime juice
1 tablespoon olive oil
1 tablespoon honey
½ tablespoon kosher salt

12 (6-inch) corn tortillas, purchased or
    homemade (page 9)
1 ripe avocado, peeled, seeded, and sliced
    lengthwise into 24 pieces
Lime wedges
Salsa of choice (see page 2)

CHO
AND
4 tal
1 po
    a
1 me
2 clo
1 jal
    r
2 dri
    t
2 tea
    N
1 lar
    ½
Kosh

12 (2
2 ou
1 cup
½ cu
    g

Brush a grid
heat until ho
(page 24) for
with ¼ cup of
spoon of gua
Pickled Onio
bled *queso fi*

GRILLED PORTOBELLO MUSHROOM TACOS
WITH SALSA PASILLA AND QUESO FRE[SCO]

Vegetarians or anyone who likes tasty, lighter fare will find these [...] a delicious choice. While these may not be a classic in Mexico, this [...] of fans among our guests in the restaurant. The Salsa Pasilla can [...] and kept in the refrigerator for up to one week.

¼ cup olive oil

2 tablespoons freshly squeezed lime juice

2 tablespoons chopped fresh cilantro leaves

1 tablespoon chopped garlic

1 serrano chile, stemmed and chopped

½ teaspoon kosher salt

½ teaspoon freshly ground black pepper

6 large portobello mushrooms, stemmed

SALSA PASILLA

4 medium whole plum tomatoes

1 small yellow onion, quartered

3 cloves garlic

6 pasilla chiles

2 chipotle chiles

2 teaspoons dark brown sugar

2 bay leaves

½ teaspoon dried oregano, preferably Mexican

½ teaspoon freshly ground black pepper

½ teaspoon ground cinnamon

½ teaspoon ground cumin

¼ teaspoon finely chopped fresh thyme leaves

¼ cup white vinegar

2 tablespoons kosher salt

12 (6-inch) corn tortillas, purchased or homemade (page 9)

1 cup very thinly sliced romaine lettuce

1 cup pico de gallo (page 2)

1 cup crumbled queso fresco

Serves 6 (12 tac[os]

In a large bowl, c[...]
garlic, chile, salt, [...]
coat evenly, and [...]

MAKE THE SALS[A...]
tomatoes, onion, [...]
for 15 to 20 minu[...]

Toast and rehydr[...]
page 6). In the ja[...]
batches, add the [...]
tomatoes, onion[s...]
salsa ingredients[...]
Add salt to taste, [...]

Heat a barbecue [...]
aluminum foil an[...]
mushrooms from [...]
Place them indiv[...]
utes, and then tu[...]
amount of time. [...]
½-inch-wide stri[...]

Serve 3 to 4 strip[s...]
with a generous [...]
gallo, 1 tablespo[...]
Salsa Pasilla. Fo[...]

WILD MUSHROOM AND HUITLACOCHE SOPES
WITH QUESO FRESCO AND TOMATILLO AVOCADO SALSA

The most difficult part of this delicious recipe is actually finding the *huitlacoche* (also spelled *cuitlacoche*). This corn fungus, also called "Mexican truffle" or "Mexican caviar," is greatly revered in Mexico. The kernels have a smoky-sweet flavor. It is best fresh or frozen, but it is also available canned from some online Mexican food suppliers (see Sources). Your best option is to purchase it frozen, but even that may be hard to find. Otherwise, try a trip to Oaxaca in the fall! If you can't find the mushrooms listed here, use portobellos or any combination of mushrooms that you like.

SOPE DOUGH (MASA)

1¼ cups corn flour for tortillas

2 tablespoons lard (see Glossary) or vegetable shortening

½ cup water

1 teaspoons kosher salt

TOMATILLO-AVOCADO SALSA

½ ripe avocado peeled, seeded, and coarsely chopped

1 cup salsa verde (page 3)

MUSHROOM-HUITLACOCHE FILLING

1 tablespoon canola oil

1 cup mixed sliced mushrooms (such as shiitake, cremini, and oyster mushrooms, but any variety may be used)

1 tablespoon unsalted butter

1 medium yellow onion, diced

2 cloves garlic, chopped

½ to 1 teaspoon ground arbol chile powder

½ cup huitlacoche (see Glossary)

1 tablespoon chopped fresh epazote (see Glossary) or a combination of flat-leaf parsley and oregano

Kosher salt and freshly ground black pepper

continued on next page

Makes 12 (2½-inch) sopes

MAKE THE SOPES: In a large bowl, mix together the corn flour, lard, water, and salt, and knead gently until the dough is smooth, about 3 minutes. Roll about 3 tablespoons of *masa* into a ball, and then flatten the ball using your thumb and the palm of your hand to form a 2½-inch-round disk, approximately ¼ inch thick. Repeat until you have 12 disks. Set aside while preparing the salsa and filling.

MAKE THE SALSA: In the jar of an electric blender, combine the avocado and salsa verde, and purée until smooth. Refrigerate until needed.

MAKE THE FILLING: Heat ½ tablespoon of the oil in a large skillet over high heat until almost smoking. Add the mushrooms and ½ tablespoon of the butter and sauté until golden brown, 3 to 5 minutes, turning often. Transfer the mushrooms to a small bowl.

In the same pan over high heat, stir in the remaining ½ tablespoon of oil along with the onion, garlic, and remaining ½ tablespoon of butter. Reduce the heat to medium and sauté until the onion is golden brown, 3 to 4 minutes. Add the chile powder, *huitlacoche*, and epazote. Cook for 2 to 3 minutes, stirring often. Return the sautéed mushrooms to the pan and cook just to heat through. Season to taste with salt and pepper. Keep warm.

Heat a griddle or large skillet over medium heat. Add 2 or 3 *masa* disks and cook for 2 to 3 minutes on each side, turning once, just to firm them slightly. Remove the disks from the pan, let them cool slightly, and then gently pinch the edges to resemble a small tart shell. Return them to the griddle, and continue cooking for 5 minutes more. Remove, wrap in aluminum foil, and keep in a warm oven.

Spoon 1 tablespoon of Tomatillo-Avocado Salsa onto each *sope*, and then add 2 tablespoons of warm mushrooms. Top with 1 teaspoon of *queso fresco*, a dollop of crema, and a sprinkle of radishes. Serve warm.

1 cup crumbled queso fresco
¼ cup crema (page 10) or sour cream
3 radishes, trimmed and cut into thin strips

CHIPOTLE-MARINATED CHICKEN FLAUTAS
WITH ROASTED CORN AND AVOCADO PICO DE GALLO

Like most flautas, which mean "flutes," this version is made with flour tortillas that are rolled around a filling, secured with toothpicks, and fried. They work well as finger food or passed appetizers at parties, and kids love them (make a milder version). They're also great to have on hand for last-minute meals, as they're easily frozen and reheated. Once rolled, flautas can be kept in a resealable plastic bag in the refrigerator for up to 24 hours or frozen for a couple of months. To make this into a full meal, serve with rice and *Frijoles Refritos* on the side (page 135).

CHIPOTLE MARINADE

4 plum tomatoes, cut in half lengthwise

1 medium-size yellow onion

4 cloves garlic

4 to 6 canned chipotle chiles in adobo

¼ cup freshly squeezed orange juice

¼ cup freshly squeezed lime juice

2 tablespoons honey

1 tablespoon kosher salt

2 pounds boneless, skinless chicken thighs

2 cups canola oil

12 (6-inch) corn tortillas, purchased or homemade (page 9)

continued on next page

TAQUITOS AND FLAUTAS

Taquitos and flautas are both small versions of tacos that are either folded or rolled and fried.

Serves 6 (12 flautas)

Preheat the oven to 400°F.

MAKE THE MARINADE: Spread the tomatoes, onion, and garlic on a metal baking pan, and roast until browned, about 15 minutes, shaking the pan occasionally. Remove the vegetables from the oven, let cool, and then transfer to the jar of an electric blender along with the remaining marinade ingredients and purée until smooth.

Put the chicken in a large mixing bowl, pour on the marinade, toss to coat well, cover, and refrigerate for at least 1 hour or overnight.

Preheat the oven to 350°F.

Lift the chicken from the marinade, and discard the marinade. Transfer the chicken to a nonreactive baking dish, cover with aluminum foil, and bake for 30 to 40 minutes, or until the chicken is cooked through and very tender. Let cool, and then shred the meat.

Heat the oil in a large skillet over medium-low heat. Carefully dip each tortilla into the oil for about 5 seconds on each side until soft and pliable and then drain and cool on paper towels. Reserve the oil.

Spoon ¼ cup of the shredded chicken across the center of each tortilla and roll up tightly, securing each end with a wooden toothpick.

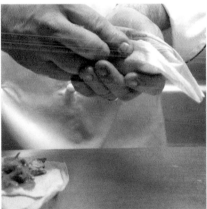

Meanwhile, heat a skillet over high heat. Add the remaining tablespoon of oil, return the meat to the pan, and brown it lightly, and then stir in 1 cup of the thickened salsa verde to moisten the mixture. Season to taste and reserve for the tamale preparation.

MAKE THE TAMALE DOUGH: While the pork is cooking, combine the corn flour, water or stock, baking powder, salt, and lard or shortening in the bowl of a stand mixer fixed with the paddle attachment. Mix at medium speed for about 3 minutes, until the tamale *masa* mixture becomes light and fluffy. Or turn out on a board with a little extra corn flour and knead until smooth.

For each corn husk, spread about a ¼ cup of *masa* into the center, and spoon about 3 tablespoons of pork in the center. Fold the corn husk according to the photos.

In a medium-size pot, bring about 2 cups of water to a simmer. Put the tamales in the water, standing each on end with the folded side down, cover, and cook for 1 hour.

Turn off the heat, and let the tamales rest for 10 to 15 minutes. Serve warm with plenty of warm thickened salsa verde and garnish with Roasted Chile *Rajas* or strips of roasted red pepper.

CORN TAMALES WITH ROASTED POBLANO CHILES AND QUESO FRESCO

This is a straightforward, inexpensive tamale recipe with puréed corn, chiles, cheese, and cilantro folded into the tamale dough. When made with shortening instead of lard, they are a good vegetarian appetizer. The garnishes and salsas that accompany the tamales may be spooned onto the dish or put in bowls and served in the center of the table.

2 poblano chiles
1 tablespoon canola oil
½ cup diced yellow onion
½ tablespoon chopped garlic
1 cup fresh corn kernels (1 to 1½ ears) or
    defrosted high-quality frozen corn
½ cup heavy cream
½ teaspoon kosher salt

continued on next page

Makes 6 tamales

Roast and peel the chiles (see page 6), and then dice them and set aside.

Heat a large skillet over medium-high heat. Add the oil and onion and sauté for 2 to 3 minutes, or until the onions are translucent, and then add the garlic and corn, and sauté for 5 minutes more. Stir in the heavy cream, season with ¼ teaspoon of the salt, and let cool, and then transfer the mixture to the jar of an electric blender and purée. Set aside.

In the bowl of a stand mixer fitted with a paddle attachment, combine the corn flour, water, lard or shortening, baking powder, and remaining ¼ teaspoon of salt, and beat on medium speed for 3 to 5 minutes, until the mixture is fluffy. Or turn out on a board with a little extra corn flour and knead until smooth. Add the corn purée and mix until blended. Gently fold in the poblano chiles, *queso fresco,* and cilantro.

Spoon about ¼ cup of dough into the center of each corn husk and fold (see the photos on page 31). In a medium-size pot, bring 2 cups of water to a simmer. Stand the tamales on end, with the folded side down, cover, and cook for 1 hour. Turn off the heat, and let the tamales rest for 10 to 15 minutes. Serve warm with salsa verde, pico de gallo, and crema.

TAMALE DOUGH (MASA)

1 cup corn flour for tamales

¾ cup warm water

⅓ cup lard (see Glossary) or solid vegetable
    shortening

½ teaspoon baking powder

1 cup crumbled queso fresco

¼ cup chopped fresh cilantro leaves

6 dried corn husks, soaked in warm water
    for 10 to 15 minutes until soft and
    pliable

1 cup salsa verde (page 3)

1 cup pico de gallo (page 2)

½ cup crema (page 10) or sour cream

DUCK CARNITAS TAMALES
WITH MOLE MANCHAMANTELES AND SOUR CHERRY SALSITA

This is a contemporary spin on traditional *carnitas* recipes in which duck is slowly braised in fat until the meat almost falls off the bone. The sauce, *Mole Manchamanteles*, translates as "tablecloth stainer," a reference to its deep red color from the red chiles. This rich, fruity *mole* from Oaxaca pairs perfectly with duck. Use the leftover *Mole Manchamanteles* for Roasted Duck Breast and Duck *Carnitas* Enchiladas (page 104). Remember, corn flour for tamales is more coarsely ground than corn flour for tortillas.

MOLE MANCHAMANTELES
MAKES 10 CUPS

3 plum tomatoes, cut in half

1 medium yellow onion, quartered

4 cloves garlic

2 tablespoons canola oil

1 small ripe plantain or banana

1 small sweet potato or yam

¼ cup slivered almonds

2 tablespoons sesame seeds

½ cup lard (see Glossary) or canola oil

5 ancho chiles, stemmed and seeded

5 guajillo chiles, stemmed and seeded

1 tablespoon dried oregano, preferably
    Mexican

1 tablespoon cumin seeds, toasted, or ½
    tablespoon ground cumin

1 tablespoon black peppercorns

2 bay leaves

1 clove

¼ cup pineapple cut into 1-inch cubes

¼ cup peeled, cored, and diced Granny
    Smith or other tart green apple

2 dried apricots

2 tablespoons golden raisins

4 cups chicken stock

continued on next page

Makes 12 tamales

MAKE THE MOLE: Preheat the oven to 400°F. Toss the tomatoes, onion, and garlic with the oil, and roast them on a baking sheet until the onion is soft and golden brown, 25 to 30 minutes. Remove and set aside.

On a baking sheet, roast the plantain and sweet potato until the plantain skin is black and bubbly, about 20 minutes, depending on the size, then continue cooking the sweet potato until soft, about 45 minutes total cooking time. Remove and let them cool. Peel both, cut into cubes, and reserve.

Toast the almonds and sesame seeds separately in a dry skillet over medium heat. Cook the almonds for 5 to 6 minutes until pale brown, and then cook the sesame seeds for 2 to 3 minutes, constantly shaking the pan to prevent burning. Set aside to cool.

Heat a medium-size skillet over medium heat. Add half of the lard or canola oil and heat until hot. Fry the chiles one at a time until they begin to bubble and darken, about 1 minute. Remove with a slotted spoon or tongs and set aside on paper towels to cool.

Combine the chiles, toasted nuts, oregano, cumin, peppercorns, bay leaves, and clove in a *molcajete*, spice grinder, or clean coffee mill and finely grind.

Combine the roasted vegetables and the ground-spice mixture with the pineapple, apple, apricots, and raisins in a large mixing bowl. Working in batches, purée the mixture in the jar of an electric blender until smooth. The mixture should be thick.

GULF RED SNAPPER CEVICHE

Huachinango is the Mexican name for the red snapper that comes from the Gulf of Mexico. It is popular for ceviche because it is mild and has a firm texture. Here it is "cooked" in freshly squeezed lime juice and then mixed with tomatillos, red onions, and serrano chiles and served with avocado purée. Scoop up this bright-tasting ceviche with tostadas (whole crispy fried tortilla rounds) or tortilla chips.

Serves 6

MAKE THE PURÉE: In the jar of an electric blender, combine all of the avocado purée ingredients except the olive oil and salt, and purée until smooth. With the blender running on low to medium speed, slowly drizzle in the olive oil until completely incorporated, and then add salt to taste. Cover and refrigerate.

MAKE THE CEVICHE: Mix the snapper, lime juice, olive oil, and salt in a nonreactive bowl and refrigerate for 1 hour. Remove from the refrigerator and stir in the tomatillos, red onion, serrano chiles, and cilantro.

MAKE THE TOSTADAS: Heat the oil in a medium-size skillet, and when hot, add the tortillas one at a time and cook until crisp, turning once, about 1 minute per side. Remove from the pan to paper towels and drain.

In small, chilled bowls, spoon in 2 tablespoons of avocado purée and then add ¼ cup of ceviche in the center. Garnish each bowl with sprigs of watercress, a tostada, and sliced avocado on the side, and serve.

ICE COLD BEER AND CEVICHE

One of my favorite recent memories is of sitting in the fish market in Ensenada. I was eating fish tacos and freshly made ceviche and drinking light Mexican beer. The beer was so cold that it almost had ice crystals in it, and I realized that very fresh ceviche and very, very cold beer is a perfect marriage.

AVOCADO PURÉE
2 ripe avocados, peeled and pitted
2 cloves garlic
½ yellow onion, peeled and quartered
½ cup loosely packed fresh cilantro leaves
½ cup water
¼ cup freshly squeezed lime juice
¼ cup rice vinegar
¼ cup olive oil
Kosher salt

CEVICHE
1 pound skinless red snapper fillets, cut into ½-inch cubes
½ cup freshly squeezed lime juice
2 tablespoons extra-virgin olive oil
1 teaspoon kosher salt
1 cup diced tomatillos
½ cup finely diced red onion
2 serrano chiles, seeded if desired, sliced crosswise into thin disks
¼ cup chopped fresh cilantro leaves

TOSTADAS
1 cup canola oil, for frying
12 (6-inch) corn tortillas, purchased or homemade (page 9)

1 bunch watercress, coarse stems removed, for garnish
1 firm, ripe avocado, peeled and sliced, for garnish

TEQUILA-CURED SALMON CEVICHE
WITH TOMATILLO PICO DE GALLO AND PAPAYA-HABANERO MUSTARD

This dish is like a cross between a Mexican-style ceviche and gravlax (sugar and salt-cured salmon). Perhaps it reveals my Swedish ancestry. The tequila and citrus in the cure mix impart a great taste, while the curing process intensifies these flavors. The acid from the tomatillos in the pico de gallo cuts the richness of the salmon, and the sweet-hot Papaya-Habanero Mustard balances the other bold flavors. For this recipe, the salmon needs to cure for 8 to 12 hours. The exact amount of time will depend on the thickness of the salmon fillet. The thicker the fish, the longer it needs to cure.

TEQUILA-CURED SALMON

1 cup kosher salt

1 cup sugar

1 orange, thinly sliced

1 lime, thinly sliced

1 lemon, thinly sliced

½ cup loosely packed fresh cilantro leaves

1 tablespoon black peppercorns

1 habanero chile, seeds and membranes removed if desired, chopped

2 pounds boneless salmon fillets with the skin on

½ cup good-quality silver tequila (see sidebar, page 197)

PAPAYA-HABANERO MUSTARD

¼ cup Dijon mustard

2 tablespoons honey

¼ cup freshly squeezed orange juice

¼ cup apple cider vinegar

continued on next page

Serves 6 to 10

PREPARE THE SALMON: In a small mixing bowl, combine the salt and sugar. In a flat, nonreactive ceramic or stainless-steel dish or pan just large enough to hold the salmon, spread half of the salt and sugar mixture to cover the bottom. Add alternating slices of oranges, limes, and lemons, using half of the fruit. Sprinkle half of the cilantro leaves, peppercorns, and habanero chile on top of the citrus and then lay the salmon fillets, skin side down, on top of the other ingredients.

Repeat the process in the reverse order, sprinkling the remaining habanero chile, peppercorns, and cilantro leaves on top of the salmon. Layer with the remaining citrus slices, and then completely cover with the remaining salt and sugar mixture. Drizzle on the tequila. Cover with plastic wrap and weigh down the mixture with another pot or pan. Refrigerate for 8 to 10 hours.

When the flesh looks opaque, remove the salmon from the cure mixture, and rinse well under cold water. Put the

RED PAPAYAS

Large, red-fleshed Caribbean papayas are about two or three times as long as their smaller, orange-fleshed cousins. They are also sweeter and harvested when green. Look for those that are firm and blemish free. Then ripen to yellow on your counter.

salmon skin side down on a plate and refrigerate uncovered for 1 hour.

MAKE THE MUSTARD: In the jar of an electric blender, combine all the ingredients for the Papaya-Habanero Mustard except for the oil and salt. Purée until smooth. With the motor running on medium speed, slowly add the olive oil, blend until smooth, and then season to taste with salt. Strain the mustard into a clean bowl and refrigerate for up to 24 hours prior to serving.

MAKE THE PICO DE GALLO: In a medium-size bowl, combine all of the ingredients for the Tomatillo Pico de Gallo, season to taste with salt, and refrigerate for at least 1 hour prior to serving.

Just before serving, slice the corn tortillas into thin strips. Heat the oil in a medium skillet over medium heat until hot and fry the tortilla strips until golden and crispy, about 2 minutes. Using a slotted spoon, remove the strips from the pan to drain on paper towels and cool.

Slice the salmon very thinly across the width of the fillet at about a 45-degree angle. Lay 3 to 5 slices in the center of each medium-size, chilled plate. Drizzle about 1 tablespoon of the Papaya-Habanero Mustard across the salmon, spoon 2 tablespoons of Tomatillo Pico de Gallo in the center, garnish with diced avocado and crispy tortilla strips, and serve.

½ cup very ripe red papaya, peeled, seeded, and cut into large cubes
½ fresh habanero chile, seeds and membranes removed, if desired
¼ cup olive oil
Kosher salt

TOMATILLO PICO DE GALLO

4 medium tomatillos, husked and finely diced
1 small red onion, finely diced
1 serrano chile, sliced into thin rings
½ cup chopped fresh cilantro leaves
2 tablespoons freshly squeezed lime juice
2 tablespoons extra-virgin olive oil
Kosher salt

2 (6-inch) corn tortillas, purchased or homemade (page 9), for crispy corn tortilla strips, or tortilla chips
1 cup canola oil, for frying
1 firm, ripe avocado, peeled and finely diced, for garnish

WILD MUSHROOM AND GRILLED NOPALES CEVICHE
WITH TOMATOES AND QUESO FRESCO

A vegetarian ceviche sounds like a contradiction, but so many of my customers want vegetarian and vegan dishes that I decided to give it a try with grilled and roasted vegetables. Nopales are cactus pads or leaves; they are often sold in Hispanic markets and increasingly in supermarkets. They are also available on the Internet (see Sources).

Serves 6 to 8

MAKE THE MARINADE: In a medium-size bowl, whisk together the sherry vinegar, lime juice, orange juice, honey, Maggi sauce, and salt, cover, and refrigerate.

To clean the cactus pads, use a large chef's knife and work with the blade parallel to each pad. Start at the top of each pad and move the blade toward the stem, using a gentle sawing motion, to remove all of the thorns. Rinse well and pat dry.

Heat a barbecue grill or broiler with the grill or pan positioned about 4 inches from the heat until hot. Brush the pads lightly with about 1 tablespoon of the olive oil, season with salt and pepper, and grill or broil each side for 2 to 3 minutes, until tender. Let cool, slice into thin strips, and refrigerate in a covered bowl.

Preheat the oven to 350°F. Toss the mushrooms with the remaining 1 tablespoon of olive oil, season with about 1 teaspoon salt and black pepper, and spoon onto a baking sheet. Bake for 10 minutes until lightly browned, remove and slice into thin strips, cover, and refrigerate.

In a large mixing bowl, combine the cactus, mushrooms, red onion, tomatoes, and oregano. Add ½ cup of the marinade, toss, and season to taste with salt and pepper.

In the center of each tostada, make a bed of ¼ cup of lettuce, top with ½ cup of the mushroom and cactus ceviche, and drizzle 1 tablespoon of the marinade over the top. Garnish each with sliced avocado and crumbled *queso fresco* and serve with bottled Mexican hot sauce.

MARINADE

½ cup sherry vinegar
¼ cup freshly squeezed lime juice
¼ cup freshly squeezed orange juice
2 tablespoons honey
1 tablespoon Maggi sauce
1 teaspoon kosher salt

2 small nopales (cactus pads)
2 tablespoons olive oil
Kosher salt and freshly ground black pepper
2 cups oyster mushrooms
2 cups shiitake mushrooms, stemmed
½ cup thinly sliced red onion
3 plum tomatoes, seeded and cut into thin strips
Pinch of oregano, preferably Mexican

6 tostadas, purchased or homemade (page 37), for garnish
1 small head romaine lettuce, cored and thinly shaved
1 firm, ripe avocado, peeled and sliced lengthwise, for garnish
1 cup crumbled queso fresco, for garnish
Mexican hot sauce of choice

TUNA CEVICHE
WITH MANGO AND SERRANO CHILE SALSA

While I was growing up, we used to vacation as a family in Ensenada, in Baja. I also went there as a Boy Scout and, during my surfing days, I slept on the beaches of Baja, so I know that the locals there catch great dorado (mahi-mahi), yellowfin tuna, and yellowtail off the coast. Because tuna loses its beautiful bright-red color and creamy texture if marinated too long, I toss it in the lime marinade and serve it immediately. Use sushi-grade raw tuna and keep the fish chilled until serving. This dish may also be spooned onto cucumber rounds, endive leaves, or tortilla chips and passed as an hors d'oeuvre.

MARINADE

1 yellow bell pepper

1 mango, peeled and cut into large chunks
  (see sidebar, page 149)

¼ cup freshly squeezed orange juice

¼ cup freshly squeezed lime juice

¼ cup rice vinegar

2 tablespoons sugar

2 teaspoons kosher salt

continued on next page

Serves 4 to 6

MAKE THE MARINADE: Roast the pepper over high heat, directly on a gas burner, over an open flame, or under the broiler, until the skin begins to blister and turn black. Use tongs to turn the pepper so that it is charred all over, even on the end. Transfer the pepper to a bowl, cover tightly with plastic wrap until cooled, and then carefully scrape off the skin. Cut a slit from the stem toward the tip and remove the seeds and membranes, and dice the pepper.

In a medium-size saucepan, combine the pepper with all of the remaining marinade ingredients, bring to a boil, and gently simmer for 10 minutes. Scrape the marinade into the jar of an electric blender and purée until smooth. Refrigerate until needed.

CEVICHES BOTH RAW AND PARTIALLY COOKED

Most ceviches are made with raw fish, but others—like those made with lobster and shrimp—are first lightly poached or steamed and then marinated. Marination time varies according to the fish. Sushi-grade tuna, for example, is marinated for only a short time because the flesh quickly breaks down and becomes opaque. Snapper and scallops take longer, but if they are left in the acidic bath too long, they will become tough.

Ceviches are often named after the region they come from, such as Veracruzana and Campechana, and they incorporate the varieties of seafood commonly found in the area. (On the Gulf of Mexico, it is common to use snapper and shrimp, since both are abundant there.) They are usually served in Mexico with saltine-like crackers, crisp round fried corn tortilla (tostadas), lime wedges, diced avocado, and bottled hot sauce.

While different varieties of seafood may be substituted in ceviche recipes, some kinds of fish are better suited for this type of preparation. These include mild, firm-fleshed, white fish, such as snapper or grouper; all shellfish (but some need to be cooked prior to marination); and all sushi-grade fish. Above all, it is essential to use the highest quality fresh seafood.

Position the rack of a barbecue or gas grill or a broiler pan about 4 inches from the heat and heat until hot. Alternatively, heat a *plancha* (griddle) until hot.

Mix the octopus with the olive oil and season to taste with salt and pepper. Grill the pieces long enough to char the flesh, 1 to 2 minutes on each side, and then remove and slice crosswise into thin rings. Combine the octopus in a medium-size bowl with 1 cup of the chile marinade, the *rajas*, and chopped oregano, and toss. Season to taste.

Spoon about 2 tablespoons of the remaining chile marinade in the center of each of 6 or 12 chilled plates, top each with ¼ cup or ½ cup (depending on whether an appetizer or entrée) of the ceviche mixture, garnish with lime wedges, tortilla chips, and romaine leaves, and serve.

OCTOPUS CEVICHE
Kosher salt
4 wine corks (optional)
⅓ cup diced onions
⅓ cup diced carrots
⅓ cup diced celery
10 peppercorns
2 bay leaves
1 lemon, cut in half
1 sprig oregano
2 pounds cleaned octopus bodies
¼ cup olive oil
Freshly ground black pepper
¼ cup chopped fresh oregano leaves

2 limes, cut into wedges, for garnish
Tortillas chips, for garnish
2 hearts of romaine lettuce, separated into
    leaves, for garnish

SEAFOOD CEVICHE CAMPECHANA
WITH TOMATO AND LIME MARINADE

MARINADE

1 cup ketchup

1 cup tomato juice

1 cup clam juice

¼ cup freshly squeezed grapefruit juice

¼ cup freshly squeezed orange juice

¼ cup freshly squeezed lime juice

1 large jalapeño chile, coarsely chopped

2 ribs celery with leaves, coarsely chopped

2 tablespoons Maggi sauce or
Worcestershire sauce

1 tablespoon Tabasco or other red hot
pepper sauce

1½ teaspoons kosher salt

1½ teaspoons freshly ground black pepper

CEVICHE

Kosher salt

2 (1-pound) lobsters, or 8 ounces cooked
lobster meat

1 pound (about 25) medium-size shrimp in
the shell

8 ounces cooked crabmeat (such as lump
crab, snow crab, or Dungeness crab)

2 to 4 jalapeño chiles, finely diced

1 cup seeded and finely diced tomatoes

½ cup finely diced red onion

½ cup chopped fresh cilantro leaves

TOSTADAS

1 cup canola oil, for frying

6 to 10 (6-inch) corn tortillas, purchased or
homemade (page 9)

2 cups guacamole (page 5)

1 cup homemade Jalapeños en Escabeche
(page 144) or purchased pickled
vegetables, cut into thin strips, for
garnish

2 cups very thinly sliced romaine lettuce
leaves, for garnish

Ceviche Campechana in a tomato-citrus marinade is named for Campeche, a town on the shore of the Gulf of Mexico. This kind of a seafood preparation is found in most coastal regions. It generally refers to a mixture of whatever fresh fish and shellfish are available that day, served in a large glass with so much marinade that it resembles a chilled soup. I use less liquid, but experiment to see what you prefer. Serve this with plenty of tostadas, lime wedges, and chopped or thinly sliced chiles.

Serves 6 to 10

MAKE THE MARINADE: In the jar of an electric blender, combine all of the marinade ingredients and purée until smooth. Pour the mixture through a strainer into a bowl, cover, and refrigerate.

MAKE THE CEVICHE: Meanwhile, in a large pot, bring 4 quarts of salted water to a boil. Add the lobsters, cover the pot, return the water to a boil, and cook for 7 minutes more, or until the shells are bright red. Remove with tongs, wrap each lobster in a piece of aluminum foil, and let cool. Reserve the cooking water.

Return the water to a boil, add the shrimp, and cook for 4 to 5 minutes, or until pink and just cooked through. Drain and let the shrimp cool, peel and devein them, and then cut them into small pieces. Shell the lobsters and cut the meat into bite-size pieces.

Toss the lobster, shrimp, and crabmeat with the jalapeño chiles, tomatoes, red onion, and cilantro. Add enough marinade to liberally coat the vegetables and mix. Season to taste with salt.

MAKE THE TOSTADAS: Heat a large skillet over medium heat. Add the oil, heat to 350°F, and then fry each tortilla until crispy and golden brown, about 1 minute per side. Remove to paper towels to drain and cool.

Spoon 2 tablespoons of guacamole on each tostada, add ¼ cup of the ceviche in the center, garnish with *Jalapeños en Escabeche* and lettuce, and serve.

CITRUS-MARINATED DIVER SCALLOP CEVICHE
WITH GRAPEFRUIT AND ORANGE SEGMENTS AND SWEET PEPPERS

The acidic taste of the citrus in this recipe plays against the sweet, creamy-textured scallops. Look for diver scallops, harvested by hand in Maine and delivered very fresh to markets and seafood stores. I use the largest-size scallops available. This recipe, like most ceviches, can also be made with many types of fish or seafood.

Serves 6

Combine the scallops with half of the three citrus juices, and refrigerate for 1 to 2 hours until opaque.

Meanwhile, in a medium-size bowl, combine the citrus segments, red and yellow peppers, cilantro, serrano chiles, and salt and gently toss with the remaining citrus juices.

Remove the scallops from the juice marinade. Set the marinade aside. Using a sharp knife, cut the scallops crosswise into ⅛ to ¼-inch-thick slices and arrange them in a circle in the center of chilled plates.

Spoon a mound of the pepper mixture in the center of the circle of scallops, spoon about 2 tablespoons of the marinating liquid over the top, garnish with slices of avocado and romaine leaves, and serve.

2 pounds diver scallops, rinsed and tendons removed
½ cup freshly squeezed lime juice
¼ cup freshly squeezed grapefruit juice
¼ cup freshly squeezed orange juice
1 cup grapefruit segments (see page 17)
1 cup orange segments (see page 17)
½ cup thinly sliced red bell pepper
½ cup thinly sliced yellow bell pepper
½ cup chopped fresh cilantro leaves
1 tablespoon thinly sliced serrano chiles
1 teaspoon kosher salt

2 firm, ripe avocados, peeled and sliced lengthwise, for garnish
Romaine lettuce leaves, for garnish

COCONUT-CITRUS-MARINATED LOBSTER CEVICHE
WITH MANGO PICO DE GALLO

This ceviche comes from the tropical region of the Yucatán, on the Caribbean coast of Mexico. Gently steamed lobster meat is marinated in a lush, tasty blend of coconut milk, citrus juices, chiles, and ginger. It is perfectly paired with a colorful pico de gallo made with mango, red onion, bell pepper, cilantro, and mint. Each portion may be divided in half for twelve appetizer portions. At the restaurant we like to garnish this dish with crispy fried green plantain chips.

CEVICHE

¾ cup canned coconut milk

¼ cup freshly squeezed lime juice

¼ freshly squeezed orange juice

¼ cup rice vinegar

1 tablespoon Thai or Vietnamese fish sauce

½ habanero chile, seeded, membrane removed, and cut lengthwise

1 tablespoon peeled and chopped fresh ginger

Kosher salt

6 (1-pound) lobsters

MANGO PICO DE GALLO

2 cups diced mango (see page 149)

1 cup diced red onion

½ cup diced red bell pepper

½ cup diced poblano chiles

1 habanero chile, seeds and membranes removed, diced

¼ cup chopped fresh cilantro leaves

¼ cup chopped fresh mint leaves

2 tablespoons freshly squeezed orange juice

2 tablespoons freshly squeezed lime juice

1 tablespoon honey

1 teaspoon kosher salt

2 green plantains, peeled, thinly sliced lengthwise, and fried, for garnish (see sidebar, page 54)

Serves 12 as an appetizer or 6 as an entrée

MAKE THE CEVICHE: In a nonreactive bowl, mix together all of the ceviche ingredients except the lobster, season with about 1 teaspoon of salt or to taste, cover, and refrigerate.

Meanwhile, in a large pot, bring at least 6 quarts of salted water to a rolling boil. Add the lobsters, cover the pot, return the water to a boil, and cook the lobsters for 7 minutes more, or until the shells are bright red. Do this in batches if the pot is not large enough to accommodate all of the lobsters. Remove the lobsters, wrap each in aluminum foil, and let cool. Cut the lobsters in half down the back and remove the tail meat. Reserve the tail shells. Break off the claws and knuckles, crack the shells, and remove the meat. Chop the meat into bite-size pieces.

MAKE THE PICO DE GALLO: In a medium-size bowl, stir together the ingredients for the Mango Pico de Gallo and set aside.

In a medium-size mixing bowl, combine the lobster meat with the other ceviche ingredients. For an appetizer, put ½ lobster tail shell in the center of each chilled plate, and fill with lobster. Garnish with Mango Pico de Gallo and crispy fried green plantain chips, and serve.

SHRIMP EMPANADAS
WITH CHIPOTLES, TOMATOES, AND CILANTRO

In these empanadas, the combination of shrimp and spicy-smoky chipotles is simply irresistible. This recipe makes a lot but I promise they'll all be eaten. Try to press as much water as possible out of the shrimp. The best way to do this is to chop the shrimp into small pieces, put them between layers of paper towels, and place a heavy weight on top for at least 20 minutes.

Makes 24 empanadas

Prepare the dough and refrigerate.

Heat a large skillet over high heat. Add 2 tablespoons of the oil and the onion and sauté until translucent, about 2 minutes, stirring frequently. Add the garlic and cook for 1 minute more. Add the tomatoes and chipotles, lower the heat to medium, and simmer until the liquid from the tomatoes evaporates, 5 or 6 minutes. Remove from the heat and let cool.

Heat a large skillet over high heat. Add the remaining tablespoon of oil and the shrimp and sauté for about 5 minutes, or until the shrimp are cooked through. Let them cool, and then drain off any water. Toss the shrimp with the tomato mixture and cilantro and season to taste with salt.

Roll the dough into 1½-inch balls, put them between two sheets of plastic wrap, and then flatten them into ⅛-inch-thick disk, using a tortilla press or between two books. Spoon 2 tablespoons of filling in the center of each disk, fold in half like a turnover, and pinch the edges to seal.

In a large saucepan, heat the oil to 350°F. Fry a few empanadas at a time—cook the first side for 2 minutes or until lightly browned, turn once, and then cook the second side for 2 minutes. Serve with Salsa Pasilla or your favorite salsa for dipping.

2 ¼ pounds dough (masa) for tortillas (page 9)

3 tablespoons olive oil

2 cups diced yellow onion

2 tablespoons chopped garlic

2 cups seeded and diced plum tomatoes

2 to 3 canned chipotle chiles in adobo, chopped

2 pounds medium shrimp, peeled, deveined, chopped, and dried

½ cup chopped fresh cilantro leaves

1 tablespoon kosher salt

4 cups canola oil, for frying

Salsa Pasilla (page 22), for dipping

ROASTED PLANTAIN EMPANADAS
WITH BLACK BEANS, SCALLIONS, AND QUESO AÑEJO

Empanadas are turnovers with a flaky crust and a spicy or sweet filling. This sweet, savory, and slightly spicy version is based on a traditional recipe from Veracruz, on the coast of the Gulf of Mexico. These can be made small for finger foods at a party or larger to serve as a plated appetizer. To make a smooth dough from plantains, choose those that feel soft to the touch and appear almost black on the outside.

When cooking the empanadas, the time can vary with the ripeness of the plantains. Riper plantains have a higher sugar content, which makes them brown and burn faster. This recipe was inspired by a similar dish at Border Grill, in Santa Monica, California, where I was formerly the chef.

DOUGH

3 large ripe plantains
1 tablespoon kosher salt

FILLING

1 tablespoons canola oil
1 small yellow onion, finely chopped
1 clove garlic, finely chopped
½ cup cooked black beans or rinsed and
   drained canned beans
¼ cup cooking liquid from the black beans
   or water, as needed
1 canned chipotle chile in adobo, chopped
Kosher salt

continued on next page

Makes 12 empanadas

Preheat the oven to 350°F. Bake the whole, unpeeled plantains on a cookie sheet until black, bubbly, and soft in the center. Remove, let cool, peel, and put in the bowl of a food processor with the salt. Mix until just smooth—do not overmix. Set aside.

MAKE THE FILLING: Heat a large skillet over medium heat. Add the oil and onion, and sauté until the onion is lightly browned, about 5 to 6 minutes. Stir in the garlic, cook 1 minute, then add the black beans, *half* of the cooking liquid or water, and the chipotle chile. Mash the beans with a potato masher or the back of a wooden spoon until chunky-smooth. Add the remaining liquid, as needed; the

PLANTAINS

Plantains are a fruit, but they are used both as a vegetable and as a fruit in Mexican cooking. Although they resemble bananas, plantains are longer and have a thicker skin. Unless the skin is completely black, they are always cooked.

Green plantains are quite starchy and taste somewhat like potatoes. At this stage, they are best boiled or fried. As the skin turns yellow, the sugar develops and they taste slightly sweet. Once the skin is totally black, the fruit is quite sweet tasting and is used in desserts.

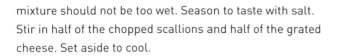

mixture should not be too wet. Season to taste with salt. Stir in half of the chopped scallions and half of the grated cheese. Set aside to cool.

Using about 3 tablespoons of the plantain dough for each disk, roll the mixture into balls. Put the balls between two sheets of plastic wrap and press the balls into disks about ⅛ inch thick, using a tortilla press or two books. Spoon 1 tablespoon of the bean-cheese mixture into the center of each disk, fold it in half like a turnover, and pinch the edges to seal.

MAKE THE AIOLI: Combine all of the aioli ingredients in a bowl and set aside.

In a large skillet, heat the oil to 350°F. Add the empanadas, a few at a time, and cook until both sides are golden brown, 1½ to 2 minutes per side. Using a slotted spoon, remove them from the pan, and drain on paper towels. Serve the empanadas hot with a dollop of Chipotle Aioli and garnish with a sprinkle of the remaining scallions and grated cheese.

¼ cup chopped scallions, including green parts

1 ounce cotija or feta cheese, finely grated (about ¼ cup)

CHIPOTLE AIOLI

1 cup prepared mayonnaise

1 tablespoon chopped canned chipotle chiles in adobo

2 tablespoons chopped scallions, including green parts

1 tablespoon honey

½ tablespoon freshly squeezed lime juice

1½ cups canola oil, for frying

BOCADITOS/Little Bites and Starters   **55**

MEXICO CITY–STYLE WILD MUSHROOM QUESADILLAS
WITH SHREDDED ROMAINE, CREMA, AND RADISHES

I call these quesadillas "Mexico City–style" because they're quite distinct from the flour tortilla turnovers filled with cheese, vegetables, or meat usually found in the United States. These are more like a giant empanada that is cooked on a griddle rather than fried. I first sampled them in Mexico City, where quesadillas are generally made with corn tortillas. Serve them with your favorite table salsa. *Queso Oaxaca* is a Mexican string cheese similar to mozzarella.

FILLING

4 tablespoon olive oil

4 tablespoons plus 1 teaspoon unsalted butter

2 cups sliced shiitake mushrooms

2 cups sliced oyster mushrooms

2 cups sliced cremini mushrooms

2 cups diced yellow onions

2 serrano chiles, seeded and thinly sliced

2 tablespoons chopped garlic

2 cups grated queso Oaxaca

½ cup loosely packed fresh epazote (see Glossary) or fresh cilantro, chopped

1 teaspoon kosher salt

2 cups dough (masa) for tortillas (page 9)

2 cups thinly shaved romaine lettuce

2 tablespoons extra-virgin olive oil

4 tablespoons red wine vinegar

¼ teaspoon kosher salt

½ cup crema (page 10) or sour cream, for garnish

6 radishes, trimmed and cut into thin strips, for garnish

Salsa of choice (see page 2)

Serves 6

MAKE THE FILLING: Heat a large skillet over medium-high heat. Add 1 tablespoon of the olive oil and 1 tablespoon of the butter, and sauté one variety of the mushrooms until golden brown, about 3 minutes. Scrape into a bowl. Repeat this process with the remaining two varieties of mushrooms, using 1 tablespoon of butter and 1 tablespoon of oil for each.

Reheat the skillet. Add the remaining 1 tablespoon of the oil and 1 tablespoon of the butter along with the onions, and sauté until lightly browned, about 5 minutes. Add the serrano chiles and garlic, cook for 2 minutes more, and then let the mixture cool. Combine the onion mixture with the mushrooms. Fold in the *queso Oaxaca* and epazote, and season to taste with salt.

Roll the dough into 2½-inch balls, put them between two sheets of plastic wrap, and press into disks measuring 6 to 8 inches in diameter and ⅛ inch thick, using a tortilla press or between two books. In the center of each disk, spoon ½ cup of the mushroom mixture, fold in half like a turnover, and pinch the edges to seal.

Warm a pancake griddle or large skillet over medium heat. Melt the remaining 1 teaspoon of butter on the griddle and then cook the quesadillas for 3 to 4 minutes per side, until they are golden and crispy and the cheese is melted.

Toss the lettuce with the olive oil, vinegar, and salt. Serve the quesadillas garnished with the romaine salad, a dollop of crema, a sprinkle of radishes, and your favorite table salsa.

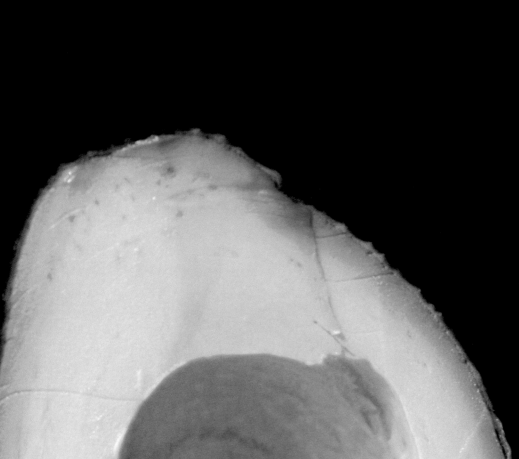

ENSALADAS Y SOPAS

Chapter Three: SALADS AND SOUPS

IN THE UNITED STATES, we love salads. We eat them simply, as a starter, or tossed with vegetables, cheese, and meat as a light entrée. In Mexico, salads are not typically served a first course and, most often, main courses are served with saladlike garnishes and vegetable side dishes. At Dos Caminos, to balance my guests' appetites for healthy lifestyle choices, I've created both appetizers and main-course salads that are very popular. Our Cobb salad is interpreted with Mexican ingredients and flavors, and we offer a very popular version of Tijuana's famous culinary gift, the Caesar.

Soups are far more prevalent in Mexican cooking than salads. I like rustic, thicker soups and stews for cold weather, and they make a very satisfying meal when served with a pile of warm corn tortillas. A famous Mexican specialty called *menudo*, or tripe soup, is renowned as a hangover cure. It sounds scary, but it has legions of fans all over Mexico and the United States.

One of my more memorable *menudo* experiences actually began with the grilled cactus salad used in the Wild Mushroom and Grilled Nopales Ceviche (page 41). A few years ago, on a trip to Atlixco, a town outside of Puebla, a group of my chefs and I visited the family of Alejandro Sanchez, my sous chef. His mother, aunt, and grandmother prepared a beautiful fiesta including the best version of *ensalada de nopalitos* that I can remember.

The festivities concluded with the music of his grandfather's mariachi band and some homemade mezcal that we drank out of two-liter Squirt bottles while we danced the night away. And, back to my original point, we had *menudo* for breakfast the next morning—and believe me, it did the trick!

The other salads and soups in this chapter are surely less intimidating and I encourage you to try them. Hopefully you will discover that their intriguing, robust flavors enliven your meals.

HEIRLOOM TOMATO SALAD
WITH CRISPY SERRANO HAM AND ROASTED CHILE AND QUESO FRESCO VINAIGRETTE

You can find heirloom tomatoes between the months of May and September at gourmet stores and farmers' markets. They come in many different colors, shapes, and sizes, all with their own distinct flavor. I recommend buying a variety of them to sample. If heirloom tomatoes are not available, choose the ripest red tomatoes you can find. Coarse sea salt sprinkled on the tomatoes adds an appealing toothsome texture.

Serves 6

MAKE THE VINAIGRETTE: In the jar of an electric blender, combine all of the vinaigrette ingredients except the olive oil and *queso fresco* and purée until smooth. With the motor running on medium speed, slowly pour in the olive oil and blend until completely incorporated. Turn off the blender, add the ½ cup of *queso fresco* and pulse until mixed. Season to taste with salt and pepper, cover, and refrigerate.

Heat a large skillet over medium heat. Add the oil and heat to 350°F. Add the ham in batches and fry until crisp, 2 to 3 minutes. Remove from the pan and drain on paper towels. Set aside.

Arrange 2 to 4 lettuce leaves in the centers of 6 chilled plates. Divide the tomatoes evenly among the plates, and sprinkle with sea salt and black pepper. Drizzle ¼ cup of the vinaigrette on the tomatoes and then sprinkle with the jalapeño chiles, red onion, and cilantro. Garnish with the remaining cup of crumbled *queso fresco* and the crispy serrano ham and serve chilled.

VINAIGRETTE

1 cup crema (page 10) or sour cream
2 tablespoons minced shallots
2 tablespoons Dijon mustard
2 roasted serrano chiles (see page 6)
2 tablespoons freshly squeezed lemon juice
¼ cup red wine vinegar
1 teaspoon minced garlic
1 teaspoon Maggi sauce or Worcestershire sauce
½ teaspoon Tabasco sauce
½ cup olive oil
½ cup crumbled queso fresco, plus 1 cup for garnish
Kosher salt and freshly ground black pepper

½ cup canola oil, for frying
½ pound thinly sliced serrano ham or prosciutto, cut into thin strips

2 to 3 heads of lettuce (such as Boston, butter, or Bibb), cored and leaves separated
2 pounds assorted heirloom tomatoes, cut into ¾-inch-thick slices
Coarse sea salt
2 to 3 large jalapeño chiles, sliced into thin rings
1 large red onion, peeled, halved, and cut into thin strips
1 cup loosely packed fresh cilantro leaves

WATERCRESS, JICAMA, AND ORANGE SALAD
WITH TOASTED PUMPKIN SEED VINAIGRETTE

In a pinch, this is a stylish, light salad that can be put together quickly. The bitterness of the watercress is balanced with the sweetness of the oranges and the creamy nuttiness of the dressing. Jicama, a root vegetable, also called "Mexican potato," is a native of that country and Central America. It looks like a large round potato, but it has a mild, sweet taste with a crunchy white interior that is similar in texture to an apple. For a variation, substitute Spiced Fresh Mango for the oranges.

Serves 6

MAKE THE VINAIGRETTE: Roast and peel the poblano chile (see page 6). Set aside.

Heat an oven or toaster oven to 350°F. In a small bowl, toss the pumpkin seeds with 1 tablespoon of the olive oil, add the chile powder and 1 teaspoon of salt, toss, and spread in a thin layer on a baking pan. Bake for 7 to 10 minutes, stirring once or twice, until golden brown. Remove and let cool.

In the jar of an electric blender, combine the poblano chile, garlic, vinegar, lime juice, and ¼ cup of the pumpkin seeds, and purée until smooth. With the motor running on medium speed, slowly pour in the remaining ¼ cup of the olive oil and the canola oil and blend until emulsified. Season to taste with salt and pepper, and chill.

In a medium-size bowl, combine the watercress, jicama, and orange segments with about 1 cup of the vinaigrette, or enough to coat the ingredients, and toss gently. Serve about 2 cups of the salad in the center of each plate. Garnish with the remaining toasted pumpkin seeds and a sprinkle of chile powder.

VINAIGRETTE

1 poblano chile
½ cup raw pumpkin seeds
¼ cup plus 1 tablespoon olive oil
½ teaspoon ancho or other chile powder, plus additional chile powder for garnish
Kosher salt
2 cloves garlic, peeled and roasted (see page 7)
¼ cup apple cider vinegar
2 tablespoons freshly squeezed lime juice
¼ cup canola oil
Freshly ground black pepper

2 to 3 bunches of watercress, large stems removed
1 jicama (about 1 pound), peeled and cut into thin strips
2 cups orange segments (see sidebar, page 17)

SPICED FRESH MANGO

Combine 3 ripe, peeled, and sliced mangoes with 2 tablespoons freshly squeezed lime juice, 2 tablespoons honey, ½ teaspoon arbol chile powder or a pinch of cayenne, ¼ cup chopped mint leaves, and a little coarse sea salt. Toss gently and serve.

QUINOA-WATERMELON SALAD
WITH ARUGULA, TOASTED PEANUTS, AND SMOKED CHILE VINAIGRETTE

Quinoa, the Incan "great grain" known to be one of the highest in protein and one of the healthiest foods on the planet, is the focus of this salad. Although both quinoa and amaranth (another important grain) are eaten in Mexico, I prefer quinoa's fluffy texture and sweet-bitter flavor. When combined with watermelon, this makes a superb summer side salad, but any fruit you like—including peaches, berries, or other melons—will work well, so long as the fruit is at its peak. Serve this salad at an outdoor barbecue or a picnic in the park. Add grilled shrimp, fish, or even chicken breast, and it becomes a healthy, well-balanced entrée.

VINAIGRETTE

1 tablespoon Dijon mustard
2 canned chipotle chiles in adobo
¼ cup freshly squeezed orange juice
¼ cup red wine vinegar
2 tablespoons honey
½ cup canola oil
Kosher salt

SALAD

2 cups quinoa
2 serrano chiles, chopped
1 large red onion, finely diced
½ cup olive oil
½ cup chopped fresh cilantro leaves
½ cup chopped fresh mint leaves
¼ cup freshly squeezed orange juice
¼ cup freshly squeezed lime juice
Freshly ground black pepper
2 cups seedless watermelon, cut into 1-inch cubes

3 cups loosely packed arugula
½ cup roasted peanuts, finely chopped, for garnish

Serves 6

MAKE THE VINAIGRETTE: In the jar of an electric blender, combine all of the vinaigrette ingredients except the oil and salt, and purée until smooth. With the motor running on medium speed, slowly add the oil until emulsified. Season to taste with about 1 teaspoon of salt, and refrigerate.

In a large pot, bring about 4 quarts of water and 1 tablespoon of salt to a boil over high heat. Add the quinoa, reduce the heat to a simmer, and cook for about 7 minutes, or until the quinoa is tender. Pour into a strainer, drain thoroughly, and spread the quinoa in a thin layer on a baking sheet to cool.

Combine the quinoa with all of the remaining salad ingredients except the diced watermelon. Mix thoroughly and season to taste with salt and pepper. Just before serving, gently fold in the watermelon.

In a medium-size bowl, toss the arugula with just enough of the vinaigrette to coat lightly. On six chilled plates, make a bed of the arugula in the center of each. Top with a ¾-cup mound of the quinoa-watermelon salad, drizzle with the remaining vinaigrette, sprinkle with the peanuts, and serve.

HEARTS OF PALM SALAD
WITH MANCHEGO CHEESE AND
ROASTED JALAPEÑO VINAIGRETTE

Many people associate hearts of palm with Mediterranean cooking, but *palmitas* are also commonly used in Mexico. Here they are combined with a spicy Roasted Jalapeño Vinaigrette. The salad bears some Spanish influences with the addition of Manchego cheese and sherry vinegar. Use a vegetable peeler to shave the cheese into long, thin strips for the garnish.

Serves 6

Roast and peel the chiles (see page 6) and finely chop.

MAKE THE VINAIGRETTE: In a large mixing bowl, whisk together the jalapeño chiles and all of the remaining vinaigrette ingredients except the olive oil, salt, and pepper. Slowly whisk in the olive oil until incorporated. Season to taste with salt and pepper, cover, and refrigerate. Mix well again before using.

Combine the mixed greens, hearts of palm, asparagus, and red onion with ½ cup of the vinaigrette and toss until well coated. Divide the salad among six chilled plates, garnish with the Manchego cheese, and serve. Any extra dressing can be refrigerated for up to 1 week.

VINAIGRETTE

1 to 3 jalapeño chiles
2 shallots, minced
1 clove garlic, chopped
½ cup sherry vinegar
2 tablespoons chopped fresh thyme leaves
1 tablespoon Dijon mustard
1 tablespoon honey
½ teaspoon dried oregano, preferably Mexican
½ teaspoon Maggi sauce or Worcestershire sauce
¾ cup olive oil
Kosher salt and freshly ground black pepper

4 cups loosely packed mixed field greens or baby lettuces
8 ounces fresh hearts of palm, or 1 (10-ounce) can, drained, sliced lengthwise in thin ribbons
12 asparagus spears, blanched and thinly sliced lengthwise into ribbons
1 small red onion, thinly sliced
4 ounces Manchego cheese, shaved into long strips, for garnish (about ½ cup)

SESAME-SEARED TUNA SALAD
WITH PINK GRAPEFRUIT SALSITA AND HABANERO-GINGER VINAIGRETTE

It is essential that you use very fresh, sushi-grade tuna in this recipe, both for health and visual reasons. For the vinaigrette, use as much or little of the habanero chile as you like because it can be intensely hot. The Pink Grapefruit Salsita's acidity lends a nice freshness to the taste.

HABANERO-GINGER VINAIGRETTE

3 shallots
2 yellow bell peppers
½ habanero chile
1 teaspoon peeled and grated fresh ginger
¼ cup freshly squeezed orange juice
¼ cup rice vinegar
1 tablespoon honey
½ cup canola oil
¼ cup sesame seeds, lightly toasted
Kosher salt

PINK GRAPEFRUIT SALSITA

1 red or yellow bell pepper, seeds and
    membranes removed, cut into thin strips
2 cups pink grapefruit segments (see
    sidebar, page 17)
1 poblano chile, seeded and cut into thin
    strips
1 medium red onion, halved and cut into thin
    strips
1 serrano chile, thinly sliced
¼ cup chopped fresh cilantro leaves
2 tablespoons olive oil
1 tablespoon honey
Kosher salt

continued on next page

Serves 6

MAKE THE VINAIGRETTE: Preheat the oven to 400°F. Roast the shallots in a lightly oiled pan until soft and lightly browned, about 10 minutes. Roast and peel the bell peppers and chile (see page 6). Set aside.

In the jar of an electric blender, combine peppers and chile with the ginger, orange juice, rice vinegar, and honey and purée until smooth. With the motor running on medium speed, slowly pour in the oil and blend until smooth. Add the sesame seeds and purée on medium speed. Season to taste with salt, and then cover and refrigerate.

MAKE THE SALSITA: In a medium-size bowl, combine all of the ingredients for the salsita. Toss gently, and season to taste with salt. Refrigerate for up to 1 hour.

Pour the sesame seeds into a flat dish. Season the tuna with salt, lightly brush with egg white, and dredge in sesame seeds until completely coated on all sides.

Heat a large heavy skillet over medium-high heat until hot. Add about 2 tablespoons of the oil and cook the tuna in batches, adding more oil as needed. Do not overcrowd the pan or the tuna will not sear properly. Sear the tuna on each side for 1 to 2 minutes for rare, or about 3 minutes for medium-rare. Remove and let rest for 1 to 2 minutes, and then slice across the grain in ¼-inch slices. The tuna may also be allowed to cool to room temperature.

In a medium-size bowl, combine the lettuce, radishes, and avocado. Add ½ cup of the vinaigrette and toss to coat the ingredients. In the center of six large, chilled plates, serve about 1 cup of the salad. Arrange 3 to 4 slices of tuna on each plate, garnish with ¼ cup of the salsita, drizzle with the vinaigrette, and serve chilled.

½ cup sesame seeds

2 pounds sushi-grade tuna steaks, cut about 1 inch thick

Kosher salt

2 large egg whites, lightly beaten

¼ cup canola oil

6 cups loosely packed mixed baby lettuces

2 cups sliced radishes

2 ripe avocados, peeled, seeded, and sliced

RED CHILE CAESAR SALAD
WITH CRISPY CALAMARI, CORNBREAD CROUTONS, AND COTIJA CHEESE

Everybody seems to love the Caesar salad, invented in Tijuana, and this version has legions of fans. Chipotle and arbol chiles impart a smoky, spicy flavor to the red chile dressing. Crispy calamari, a huge favorite with our guests, is optional.

2 cups cubed Cornbread (page 184)
2 tablespoons extra-virgin olive oil
1 teaspoon chile powder

RED CHILE CAESAR DRESSING
2 to 4 anchovy filets
2 cloves garlic
2 canned chipotles chiles in adobo
1 arbol chile
1 large egg yolk
¼ cup red wine vinegar
¼ cup freshly squeezed lemon juice
2 tablespoons Dijon mustard
½ teaspoon Worcestershire sauce
½ teaspoon Maggi sauce
¼ teaspoon Tabasco sauce
1 cup canola oil
4 ounces cotija or feta cheese, grated, plus
    4 ounces for garnish (about 1 cup total)
Kosher salt and freshly ground black
    pepper

CALAMARI
12 ounces cleaned squid bodies, cut into
    thin rings
1 cup buttermilk
2 cups canola oil, for frying
1 cup all-purpose flour
½ cup yellow cornmeal
½ teaspoon kosher salt
Pinch of ancho chile powder

 3 to 4 hearts of romaine, cored and broken
    into bite-size pieces (8 to 9 cups)

Serves 6

PREPARE THE CORNBREAD. Reserve the remaining cornbread in a resealable plastic bag and refrigerate for a few days to eat later. Preheat the over to 350°F. Toss the cornbread cubes with the olive oil and chile powder, transfer them to a baking sheet, and bake for 8 to 10 minutes, until crispy, turning once or twice. Let cool.

MAKE THE DRESSING: In the jar of an electric blender, add all of the dressing ingredients except the oil, cheese, salt, and pepper, and purée until smooth. With motor running on medium speed, slowly pour in the oil and blend until the dressing is emulsified. Pour into a bowl, add ½ cup of the *cotija* cheese, and season to taste with salt and pepper. Set aside.

MAKE THE CALAMARI: In a small bowl, combine the squid rings and buttermilk, and toss to coat. Immediately transfer the rings to a strainer to drain the excess liquid.

Heat the oil in a deep, medium-size pan to 350°F.

In a flat dish or pie plate, combine the flour, cornmeal, salt, and chile powder. Working in batches, toss the squid rings in the dry ingredients. Transfer to a strainer and shake gently to remove excess flour, and then add to the hot oil. Do not crowd the squid pieces. Cook until the rings are golden brown, 2 to 3 minutes, remove with a slotted spoon to paper towels to drain, and continue to cook the remaining squid.

In a large bowl, toss the romaine with 1 cup of the dressing. Fold in the cornbread and the remaining ½ cup of *cotija* cheese, toss again, and serve in chilled bowls. Remaining dressing may be refrigerated for a week.

DOS CAMINOS CHOPPED SALAD

This salad works well either as an appetizer or as a light main course for anyone who likes the bold flavors of Mexican food. If you add a pound of grilled chicken breast strips or shrimp to the salad, it becomes a more substantial entrée. At Dos Caminos, it is our number one appetizer next to guacamole.

Serves 4 to 6

Heat the oil in a small skillet over high heat. Add the corn, and quickly sauté until the kernels are lightly browned, shaking the pan frequently, 2 to 3 minutes. Remove and set aside.

Roast and peel the chiles (see page 6), then dice and combine them in a large bowl with the lettuce, apple, tomatoes, onion, beans, olives, cilantro, and cheese. Toss to blend.

MAKE THE VINAIGRETTE: Heat the cumin seeds in a small skillet over medium heat for about 2 minutes, shaking the pan often, to prevent burning and to release their aroma and flavor. Transfer to a spice grinder, and grind into a fine powder.

Combine the cumin, egg yolk, vinegar, and mustard in the jar of an electric blender or in a medium-size bowl. With the motor running on medium speed, slowly add the oil, and blend until emulsified. If mixing by hand, slowly pour in the oil while whisking constantly to create a thick dressing. Season to taste with salt and pepper.

Heat the oil in a deep, medium-size pan over medium-high heat until hot, about 350°F on an instant-read thermometer. Add the tortilla strips in batches and cook until golden brown, 1 to 2 minutes. Remove with a slotted spoon to paper towels to drain.

Pour about two-thirds of the vinaigrette over the salad, toss to blend, adding more, if desired. Divide the salad among four or six plates, garnish with crispy tortilla strips, and serve. Pass extra vinaigrette at the table.

NOTE

Poblano and Anaheim chiles are both fresh green chiles. They are typically sold side by side in markets, but Anaheims are long, skinny, and pale green, while poblanos are short and stout (see Glossary).

2 teaspoons canola oil

¾ cup fresh corn kernels (about 1 ear) or detrosted high-quality frozen corn or canned corn

2 poblano or Anaheim chiles, or ½ cup canned green chiles

1 head romaine lettuce, cored, washed, and chopped (4 cups)

1 small Granny Smith apple, peeled, cored, and diced (½ cup)

½ cup diced plum tomatoes

½ cup diced red onion

½ cup canned pinto beans, rinsed and drained

½ cup Spanish green olives without pimentos, sliced

¼ cup chopped fresh cilantro leaves

1 ounce cotija or feta cheese, finely grated (about ¼ cup)

VINAIGRETTE

2 tablespoons cumin seeds, or 1 tablespoon ground cumin

1 large egg yolk

½ cup red wine vinegar

1 tablespoon Dijon mustard

1 cup olive oil or canola oil

Kosher salt and freshly ground black pepper

1 cup canola oil, for frying

4 (6-inch) corn tortillas, purchased or homemade (page 9), cut into thin strips, or purchased crispy fried tortilla chips, for garnish

ENSALADA NOCHE BUENA
CHRISTMAS EVE SALAD

This colorful salad of beets and pomegranate seeds set off by deep green watercress and baby lettuces is a staple of Christmas Eve feasts in Mexico. The optional creamy goat cheese or *queso fresco* adds a contemporary touch. Although a holiday specialty, this salad is refreshing during any season the ingredients are available.

2 medium-size red beets, trimmed

½ cup golden raisins

½ cup pine nuts

6 cups baby lettuces, watercress, or arugula or a mixture of all three

1 small (about 1-pound) jicama, peeled and cut into thin strips

2 Valencia or Navel oranges, peeled and cut into segments (see sidebar, page 17)

CITRUS-JALAPENO VINAIGRETTE

¼ cup red wine vinegar

¼ cup freshly squeezed orange juice

2 tablespoons freshly squeezed lime juice

1 tablespoon Dijon mustard

2 tablespoons honey

1 jalapeño chile, seeded and minced

½ cup olive oil

Kosher salt and freshly ground black pepper

Seeds from 1 pomegranate (about ½ cup)

½ cup coarsely chopped fresh cilantro leaves

4 ounces goat cheese or queso fresco, crumbled (about 1 cup) (optional)

Serves 4 to 6

Preheat the oven to 375°F. Wrap each beet in a piece of aluminum foil and place on a baking sheet. Roast the beets until very tender when pierced with the tip of a knife, 40 to 45 minutes. Remove the pan from the oven, let the beets cool completely, unwrap, and then use a clean, old towel (one that you don't mind getting stained red) or sturdy paper towels to rub off the skin. Cut the beets into thin strips.

While the beets are cooking, cover the raisins with warm water in a small bowl and let them stand for 10 minutes until plumped. Drain and blot dry.

Preheat a toaster oven to 350°F. Toast the pine nuts in the baking tray for 4 to 5 minutes, until golden brown, shaking the pan occasionally and watching that they don't burn. Set aside. Alternatively, cook in a skillet over medium-high heat, shaking the pan often.

In a large bowl, combine the lettuce with the beets, raisins, jicama, and orange segments. Toss gently to mix.

MAKE THE VINAIGRETTE: In a small bowl, whisk together the vinegar, orange and lime juices, mustard, honey, and jalapeño chile. Add the olive oil, salt, and pepper and whisk vigorously until emulsified. Immediately pour about half of the vinaigrette over the salad, and toss gently.

Arrange the salad on a serving platter or individual plates and top with the pine nuts, pomegranate seeds, cilantro, and cheese. Serve immediately and pass the remaining dressing at the table.

FELIZ NAVIDAD/MERRY CHRISTMAS

Christmastime in Mexico is an unforgettable and delicious season of celebrations. Like most Mexican holidays, it revolves around family and food.

Navidad festivities begin on December 16 with nine days of *las posadas,* candlelit processions reenacting Mary and Joseph's journey from Nazareth to Bethlehem looking for shelter. (*Posada* means "shelter" or "lodging" in Spanish.) In each neighborhood, friends gather for food and drink in the late afternoon at the home of one family. Around dusk, the parade begins, with a young girl dressed as the Virgen María, sometimes seated atop a burro, and a little boy as San José. Other children are colorfully costumed as the Three Kings and as shepherds and shepherdesses, complete with walking staffs and paper lanterns. Their parents and the musicians follow.

DOS CAMINOS COBB SALAD

I decided to tweak the traditional Cobb salad, replacing bacon with Mexican chorizo and gorgonzola with *queso fresco* and tossing it with Cilantro-Basil Vinaigrette. It is one of our most popular entrée salads.

CILANTRO-BASIL VINAIGRETTE

1 cup loosely packed fresh basil leaves
1 cup loosely packed fresh cilantro leaves
1 shallot, chopped
1 teaspoon minced garlic
1 jalapeño chile, chopped
½ cup rice vinegar
¼ cup freshly squeezed lime juice
¼ tablespoon honey
¾ cup canola oil
Kosher salt

1 cup canola oil, for frying
4 (6-inch) corn tortillas, purchased or
    homemade (page 9), cut into thin strips,
    or purchased fried tortilla chips

SALAD

1 tablespoon canola oil
2 cups fresh corn kernels (about 3 ears) or
    defrosted high-quality frozen corn
2 heads romaine lettuce, outer leaves
    removed, chopped
2 firm, ripe avocados, peeled and diced
2 cups peeled, seeded, and diced plum
    tomatoes
1 cup finely diced red onion
1 pound queso fresco, cut into small cubes
2 pounds chorizo links, roasted and sliced
    thin on a bias
2 pounds chicken breasts, grilled and diced

Serves 6

MAKE THE VINAIGRETTE: In the jar of an electric blender, combine all of the ingredients for the vinaigrette except the oil and salt, and purée until smooth. With the motor running on medium speed, slowly add the canola oil and blend until the dressing is emulsified. Season to taste with salt and refrigerate. Mix well before using.

Heat the oil in a deep, medium-size pan over medium-high heat until hot, about 350°F on an instant-read thermometer. Add the tortilla strips in batches and cook until golden brown, 1 to 2 minutes. Remove with a slotted spoon to paper towels to drain.

Heat a medium skillet over medium-high heat until hot. Add the oil and corn and cook until the kernels are lightly browned and tender, shaking the pan occasionally, 4 to 5 minutes.

Divide the romaine among six chilled bowls or plates. Arrange equal amounts of corn, avocado, tomato, and onion attractively on top of the romaine. Add the tortilla strips, *queso*, chorizo, and chicken and serve with the vinaigrette on the side.

CUCUMBER AND TOMATILLO GAZPACHO
WITH SERRANO CHILES, YERBA BUENA, AND CREMA

In this version of the very popular Spanish cold soup, I use tomatillos rather than to-matoes. They have a slightly higher, refreshingly acidic taste. The flavor of the soup is enhanced with *yerba buena*, or spearmint, popular in Mexican cooking (see Glossary). Unlike what's usually served here in the United States, this gazpacho is blended until smooth. As a variation, you might add one cup of fresh crabmeat.

Serves 6

In the jar of an electric blender, combine the 2 chopped cucumbers, tomatillos, onion, garlic, 2 chopped serrano chiles, water, bread cubes, ½ cup of the *yerba buena*, and cilantro and purée until just smooth. Do not overblend or the color will darken from the heat caused by the friction. With the blender running on medium speed, drizzle in the olive oil, and blend until smooth. Season to taste with salt, cover, and refrigerate until well chilled.

Ladle 1 cup of the gazpacho into each of six chilled soup bowls. Sprinkle about 1 tablespoon each of the remaining cucumber, red onion, bell pepper, and jicama around the bowl. Finish with 2 to 3 slices of serrano chile, a sprinkle of fresh *yerba buena*, and a drizzle of crema.

2 medium cucumbers, peeled, seeded, and cut into small chunks, plus 1 peeled, seeded, and finely diced cucumber, for garnish

6 tomatillos, husked

1 medium-size yellow onion, coarsely chopped

4 cloves garlic, coarsely chopped

2 serrano chiles, coarsely chopped, plus 2 serrano chiles sliced into thin rings, for garnish

4 cups water

1 cup stale bread cubes with crusts removed

½ cup loosely packed fresh yerba buena or spearmint leaves, plus ¼ cup for garnish

½ cup loosely packed fresh cilantro leaves

¼ cup olive oil

Kosher salt

1 small red onion, peeled and finely diced, for garnish

1 red bell pepper, seeds and membranes removed, finely diced, for garnish

½ cup peeled, finely diced jicama, for garnish

½ cup crema (page 10) or sour cream, for garnish

SOPA DE ELOTE CON CALABAZA
CORN SOUP WITH ZUCCHINI AND OAXACAN CHEESE QUESADILLA

The optimal time to enjoy this light soup is when fresh corn is at its peak. Zucchini makes it colorful, and epazote (see Glossary) imparts a unique oregano-like flavor. If possible, buy the herb fresh in Hispanic markets, or you can substitute the dried form. Crispy, crunchy quesadillas make this similar to that classic American combo—soup and a grilled cheese sandwich. The quesadillas can be made ahead and reheated on a griddle or in a buttered skillet.

1 large poblano chile
2 tablespoons canola oil
1 medium-large yellow onion, chopped
2 cloves garlic, minced
2 cups fresh corn kernels (3 to 4 ears) or defrosted high-quality frozen corn
4 cups chicken stock
2 sprigs fresh epazote, or 1 teaspoon dried epazote or oregano
1 bay leaf
Kosher salt and freshly ground black pepper
2 cups (1 medium) diced zucchini

QUESADILLAS
6 ounces queso Oaxaca, mozzarella, or Monterey Jack cheese, shredded (about 1½ cups)
1 serrano chile, chopped
½ cup chopped fresh cilantro leaves
6 (6-inch) purchased flour tortillas
2 tablespoons unsalted butter, at room temperature
6 limes wedges, for garnish

Serves 6

Roast the chile (see page 6), dice, and set aside.

In a large soup pot, heat 1 tablespoon of the oil over medium heat. Add the onion, and sauté until translucent, about 5 minutes. Add the garlic and 1 cup of the corn kernels, and cook for 5 minutes more.

Add the chicken stock, epazote, bay leaf, salt, and pepper, and simmer gently for 15 to 20 minutes. Transfer the mixture in batches to the jar of an electric blender or food processor and purée until smooth.

In a clean pot, heat the remaining tablespoon of oil over medium-high heat. Add the remaining 1 cup of corn, the poblano chile, and the zucchini, and sauté for 5 minutes, or until the vegetables are lightly browned. Stir in the soup mixture and bring to a simmer.

MAKE THE QUESADILLAS: Sprinkle the shredded cheese, chile, and ¼ cup of the cilantro on half of each tortilla. Fold each tortilla in half and spread the outsides with softened butter. Heat a skillet over medium-high heat. Add the quesadillas and fry until golden brown and crispy, about 2 minutes, and then turn and cook the second side until brown. Remove and cut each into 4 pieces.

Ladle the soup into six large bowls and garnish with the remaining cilantro and the lime wedges. Serve with the quesadillas.

ROASTED PUMPKIN AND ANCHO CHILE SOUP
WITH TOASTED PUMPKIN SEEDS AND SPICED CREMA

Spiced crema and toasted pumpkin seeds are two great additions to this flavorful pumpkin soup. If you can find a smaller sugar pumpkin, also called a "pie pumpkin," it is a great choice for this soup because it has more meat and a more intense flavor than most pumpkins. Use an extra (hollowed out) pumpkin for a dramatic and very appropriate serving tureen.

Serves 8

Preheat the oven to 375°F.

Cut the pumpkin or squash in half lengthwise. Remove the seeds and reserve them for the Spiced Pumpkin Seeds.

Put the pumpkin on a baking sheet, cut side up. To each half, add 2 tablespoons of the butter and 2 tablespoons of the *piloncillo*. Sprinkle each half with a pinch of the spices and some salt, cover with aluminum foil, and bake for 30 to 40 minutes until the flesh is soft and slightly brown. (Bake the pumpkin seeds at the same time as the pumpkin.) Remove and let cool. With a large spoon, scoop out the flesh and discard the outer skin. Set aside.

Heat a large, heavy-bottomed pot over medium-high heat. Add the olive oil and onion, and sauté until translucent, about 3 minutes. Add the chiles and garlic and cook 2 minutes more. Add the remaining 4 tablespoons *piloncillo* and the pumpkin, stir in the chicken stock, orange juice, the remaining spices, and the bay leaves. Bring the soup to a slow boil, and then reduce the heat to a gentle simmer and cook for 20 minutes. Remove the bay leaves and working in batches, purée the soup in the jar of an electric blender until smooth. Pour the soup through a fine strainer, stir in the heavy cream, and season to taste with salt. If necessary, return the soup to the pan and gently reheat.

MAKE THE CREMA: In a small bowl, stir together all of the ingredients for the Spiced Crema with ½ teaspoon salt and refrigerate until needed.

Ladle the hot soup into bowls. Add a dollop of crema and some Spiced Pumpkin Seeds and serve.

1 (2-pound) sugar pumpkin or butternut squash, or 3 cups canned pumpkin
4 tablespoons unsalted butter
½ cup finely chopped *piloncillo* or firmly packed dark brown sugar
½ teaspoon ground cinnamon
¼ teaspoon ground allspice
¼ teaspoon ground nutmeg
Kosher salt
2 tablespoons olive oil
1 large yellow onion, coarsely chopped
3 ancho chiles, seeded and coarsely chopped
2 cloves garlic, chopped
4 cups chicken stock or water
½ cup freshly squeezed orange juice
2 bay leaves
½ cup heavy cream

SPICED CREMA
1 cup crema (page 10) or sour cream
2 tablespoons honey
2 tablespoons freshly squeezed orange juice
Pinch of ground cinnamon
Pinch of allspice
Pinch of nutmeg
½ cup Spiced Pumpkin Seeds (page 51) or toasted pumpkin seeds, for garnish

SOPA AZTECA
CHICKEN AND TORTILLA SOUP

The heat of the chiles and chicken soup's well-known nurturing goodness make this a dish to warm your body and soul. Roasted tomatoes puréed with chiles and crisp tortilla chips make this hearty enough for lunch on a cold day. Add more chicken for heartier appetites. Like most soups, this tortilla soup is better on the second day, after the flavors have blended.

Serves 4 to 6

Preheat the oven to 400°F.

In an oven-safe baking dish, toss the tomatoes with 1 tablespoon of the olive oil, sprinkle with salt and pepper, and roast for about 15 minutes, until the skin is brown and blistered. Remove and let cool.

Toast the guajillo and pasilla chiles (see page 6), and then let them cool.

In a large soup pot, heat the remaining 1 tablespoon olive oil over medium heat. Add the onion and sauté until translucent, about 5 minutes, and then add the garlic and cook for 2 to 3 minutes more, or until the onions and garlic are soft. Stir in the roasted tomatoes, chiles, bay leaf, and chicken stock, and simmer for 20 minutes. Remove the bay leaf, add half the tortilla chips, and purée the soup in batches in a food processor or an electric blender until smooth. Season to taste with salt and pepper. Return the soup to the pot and reheat if necessary.

Divide the soup among six wide soup bowls. Add the avocado, chicken, *queso fresco,* and cilantro, along with a sprinkle of the remaining tortilla chips. Or serve the garnishes separately in small bowls so guests may add as much or as little as they choose.

6 plum tomatoes, cut in half lengthwise

2 tablespoons olive oil

Kosher salt and freshly ground black pepper

2 guajillo chiles

2 pasilla chiles

1 medium-size yellow onion, coarsely chopped

4 cloves garlic, chopped

1 bay leaf

4 cups chicken stock

2 cups broken corn tortilla chips, plus extra for garnish

1 ripe avocado, peeled, seeded, and cut into ½-inch cubes

8 ounces boneless, skinless chicken breasts, grilled and cut into ½-inch cubes

4 ounces queso fresco, cut into ½-inch cubes

¼ cup chopped fresh cilantro leaves

SOPA DE ALBONDIGAS
MEXICAN MEATBALL SOUP WITH CHAYOTE AND ROASTED CORN IN RED CHILE-TOMATO BROTH

When we think of meatballs, most people think Italian. But this soup shows otherwise. Meatball soup is one of the most traditional soups in Mexico, and it is dearly loved. Vegetables, meatballs, and cheese are spooned in the bottom of soup bowls with the boiling hot broth ladled over them. Chayote is a smallish, pale green squash with smooth, slightly ridged skin. Although similar to zucchini, it has a firmer texture that requires longer cooking.

ALBONDIGAS/MEATBALLS

2 tablespoons canola oil

1 small yellow onion, finely diced

2 cloves garlic, chopped

1 medium tomatillo, husked and finely diced (about ⅓ cup)

1 serrano chile, chopped

½ pound ground beef

½ pound ground pork

1 large egg, lightly beaten

½ cup Japanese breadcrumbs (panko) or Italian seasoned breadcrumbs

¼ cup chopped fresh cilantro leaves, plus ¼ cup for garnish

Kosher salt and freshly ground black pepper

ROASTED TOMATO-CHIPOTLE BROTH

1 tablespoon olive oil

1 small yellow onion, coarsely chopped

2 cloves garlic, coarsely chopped

2 plum tomatoes, roasted and chopped (see page 7)

1 to 2 canned chipotle chiles in adobo

1½ cups chicken stock

1 bay leaf

1 tablespoon chopped fresh hoja santa, or 1 teaspoon dry

¼ teaspoon oregano, preferably Mexican

continued on next page

Serves 4 generously

MAKE THE ALBONDIGAS: Heat a large, heavy skillet over medium heat. Add ½ tablespoon of the oil and the onion and gently sauté until translucent, about 3 minutes, stirring occasionally. Add the garlic, sauté for 1 minute more, and then stir in the tomatillos and serrano chile. Lower the heat to medium-low, and sauté for 5 minutes more until the mixture is reduced. Set aside to cool.

Preheat the oven to 350°F. Lightly grease a baking sheet.

In a large bowl, combine the ground meats. Make a well in the center, and add the tomatillo mixture, the egg, the breadcrumbs, and ¼ cup of the cilantro. Season with about 1 teaspoon of salt and pepper to taste, and gently mix until combined. Roll the mixture into 1-inch balls and bake on the baking sheet for 7 or 8 minutes until just cooked through. Remove and let cool. Set aside.

MAKE THE BROTH: Heat a large, heavy-bottomed pot over medium-high heat. Add the olive oil and onion and sauté until translucent, about 3 minutes. Add the garlic and sauté for 1 minute. Stir in the tomatoes and chipotles, and cook for 2 minutes more.

Add the chicken stock, bay leaves, *hoja santa*, oregano, and salt to taste, and bring to a simmer over medium heat. Reduce the heat to low and gently simmer for 15 minutes. Remove the bay leaf and transfer the mixture in batches to the jar of an electric blender and purée until smooth. Strain into a clean pan and keep hot.

In a large skillet over medium heat, heat 1 tablespoon of the remaining canola oil from the meatballs. Add the meatballs in batches, taking care not to crowd the pan. Brown all sides and cook until heated through, 2 to 3 minutes.

Heat a small skillet over medium-high heat. Add the remaining ½ tablespoon of oil and the corn kernels, and sauté until the corn is lightly browned and heated through, 4 to 5 minutes, shaking the pan occasionally.

Divide the chayote and corn among four wide, large, warmed soup bowls. Spoon 4 to 6 meatballs into each bowl and the same amount of *queso fresco*. Ladle the hot broth over the meatballs, garnish with the remaining ¼ cup of cilantro, and serve.

½ cup diced chayote, blanched, peeled, and cut into small cubes

½ cup roasted corn kernels cut from the cob or high-quality defrosted frozen corn

½ pound queso fresco, cut into small cubes

HOJA SANTA

Hoja santa, also known as "root beer plant," is widely used by cooks in southern Mexico. The aromatic herb, also known as "sacred leaf or herb," is often used to season Mexican dishes, including *mole verde*. The taste is reminiscent of anise. The large leaf is sometimes used to wrap foods like tamales, fish, or poultry. If you cannot find it, substitute fresh tarragon leaves.

MENUDO CON POZOLE

Anyone who has been to Mexico knows that *menudo* is their celebrated traditional tripe soup—not the boy band. It is served with *pozole*, the Spanish word for "hominy." This well-known cure for hangovers is most commonly served on weekends, when that sorry state most often occurs. Typically, extra Mexican oregano and sliced fresh jalapeños are offered on the side as a garnish.

4 guajillo chiles

2 arbol chiles

¼ cup apple cider vinegar

1 teaspoon salt

2 pounds honeycomb tripe, diced pork shoulder, or chicken

2 tablespoons olive oil

1 large yellow onion, finely diced

1 tablespoon chopped garlic

½ cup peeled and finely diced carrots

½ cup finely diced celery

8 cups high-quality chicken stock

½ teaspoon dried oregano, preferably Mexican

4 bay leaves

Kosher salt

4 cups canned pozole or white hominy, drained

12 to 18 (6-inch) corn tortillas, purchased or homemade (page 9), warmed

½ cup finely diced red onion, for garnish

2 limes, cut into 12 wedges, for garnish

2 jalapeño chiles, thinly sliced crosswise, for garnish

Dried oregano, preferably Mexican, for garnish

Serves 6 to 8

Toast and rehydrate the guajillo and arbol chiles (see page 6). Let cool, and reserve the liquid. In the jar of an electic blender, combine the chiles, vinegar, salt, and only as much cooking liquid as possible to make a smooth paste.

Rinse and scrub the tripe in warm salty water, changing the water 2 or 3 times until clean. Cut into 1-inch squares. Set aside.

Heat a large, heavy pot over medium heat. Add the oil and onion and sauté until translucent, about 3 minutes. Add the garlic, carrots, and celery, and cook for 5 minutes more. Add the tripe, chicken stock, puréed chiles, oregano, bay leaves, and about 2 teaspoons of salt. Bring the liquid to a simmer and cook for 1 hour, or until the tripe is tender. Stir in the hominy and taste to adjust the seasonings.

Serve the soup very hot with warm corn tortillas and garnished with red onion, lime wedges, jalapeño chiles, and a sprinkling of oregano.

NOTE

For non-tripe lovers, the soup can also be made with pork or chicken. If using pork, cook diced pork shoulder or butt in place of the tripe. If using chicken, add diced fresh breast or boneless thigh meat to the soup and simmer for 15 minutes.

BLACK BEAN
AND CHORIZO CHILI

We serve this chili with our Chipotle-Barbecued Ribs (page 116), but you might also enjoy it over grilled cheese sandwiches, on baked potatoes, or simply in a large bowl with lots of chopped onions. Our unique version—made with bacon, chorizo, chiles, and a complex blend of spices—has layers of intense tastes.

      This recipe makes about a gallon of chili, so it is perfect for a backyard barbecue or Super Bowl Sunday. I recently served it at Giants Stadium for a tailgate party with *Arrachera*/Grilled Marinated Skirt Steak (page 106) and Chipotle-Barbecued Ribs. Leftovers may be kept in the refrigerator for up to 5 days or frozen for 1 to 2 months, then defrosted, and reheated until hot. Of course, you can cut the recipe in half, but why? You and your friends are sure to devour the whole recipe in a sitting or two.

Serves 12 or more

Toast and rehydrate the ancho chiles and purée them with the chipotle chiles into a smooth paste (see page 6).

Heat the oven to 400°F. Put the tomatoes on an oiled baking sheet and roast them until the skins are blistered, 15 to 30 minutes. Remove, cool, and chop.

Cook the bacon in a large, heavy pot over medium-high heat until the pieces are brown. Remove from the pan with tongs and drain on paper towels. Heat the bacon fat remaining in the pan over medium-high heat. Add the chorizo and, using a spoon or wooden spatula, break up the pieces and cook until the meat is brown. Drain all but 2 tablespoons of the fat.

Add the onion and garlic and cook until soft, 5 to 6 minutes. Return the bacon to the pan, add the chili purée, chopped tomatoes, bay leaves, cumin, oregano, and anise, and cook for 5 minutes. Stir in the chicken stock and beer, add the black beans, and bring the mixture to a simmer. Cook for 40 minutes, stirring occasionally. Season to taste with salt and pepper. Serve garnished with sliced scallions.

4 ancho chiles

2 canned chipotle chiles in adobo, chopped

4 plum tomatoes

½ pound applewood-smoked bacon or other thick-sliced bacon, chopped

1 pound Mexican chorizo, casings removed, crumbled

1 tablespoon canola oil

1½ cups finely diced yellow onion

2 tablespoons chopped garlic

4 bay leaves

2 tablespoons cumin seeds, toasted and ground, or 1 tablespoon ground cumin

1 teaspoon dried oregano, preferably Mexican

½ teaspoon ground anise

3½ quarts chicken stock

¾ cup light Mexican beer, such as Tecate

3 cups cooked black beans or rinsed and drained canned black beans

Kosher salt and freshly ground black pepper

Sliced scallions, for garnish

PLATOS PRINCIPALES

Chapter Four: MAIN COURSES

MY FONDEST MEMORIES OF Mexico inspired

many of these main courses, especially the dishes with the incredibly complex-tasting *mole* sauces. These are probably Mexico's most significant contribution to world cuisine. After spending many days learning about and mostly eating the numerous renditions of these awesome sauces in Oaxaca, Puebla, and other cities, I've concluded that the flavor of a great *mole* sauce can rival the finest sauce in any cuisine. That said, every Oaxacaño and Poblano thinks that his or her version is the original and the best! Having witnessed many battles over these sauces, I have to be diplomatic and say both places have some of the best food known to man.

Making *mole* is often time-consuming, so it is generally prepared for holidays and celebrations in Mexico. But if you invest the time and effort, you will be rewarded. I've included several *mole* sauces in this book. Two famous *moles* from Oaxaca are *Mole Coloradito*, or "little red *mole*," and *Mole Manchamanteles*, the fruity, bright red *mole* that translates as "tablecloth stainer" that is used here with Roasted Duck Breast and Duck *Carnitas* Enchiladas, as well as in chapter 2. *Mole Poblano*, the famous black *mole* from Puebla, turns a simple roast turkey into a spectacular centerpiece, as it does in Ancho-Rubbed Roasted Turkey with *Mole Poblano*.

Lamb *Barbacoa* is another dish that can incite a riot between these two fantastic cities. It's also the sort of dish that dreams are made of. Each Sunday, when the cooks at La Capilla restaurant in Zaachilla, outside of the city of Oaxaca, remove the steaming hot roasted lamb wrapped in banana leaves from the pit, a huge crowd waits with their mouths watering to savor the intensely fragrant, meltingly tender meat.

The first time I made *Cochinita Pibil*, a large pig slathered with achiote paste, wrapped in banana leaves, and roasted in a pit, I was in the middle of the Yucatán jungle with the leading Mexican authority on how to prepare this classic dish. It was served with fiery hot habanero chiles and plenty of ice cold *cerveza* (beer). I can't remember many other dishes that tasted better than this.

Many people don't realize that Mexico has some of the most pristine waters and some of the best fish and shellfish in the world. My travels have taken me to the coastal cities of Playa del Carmen, Veracruz, and Campeche, as well as to the Baja Peninsula to towns like Ensenada and Cabo San Lucas, and many towns in between. I've eaten astounding seafood stews and some of the best shrimp you will ever taste, and I've had *Pescado Veracruzano*—Veracruz's famous fish dish—in every outpost in this state along the coast of the Gulf of Mexico.

My interpretations of many of these dishes are in this chapter.

AVOCADO LEAF–CRUSTED TUNA
WITH SPICY PAPAYA SALSA

Dried avocado leaf has a distinctive anise flavor that is used in Mexico like a bay leaf
in soups, sauces, and stock. It is traditionally added during cooking and then removed
before serving. For this recipe, however, I use ground leaves as a crust for tuna. Green
papaya—a young Mexican red papaya—adds a crunchy texture and a less-sweet, more-
acidic flavor. The leaves harvested from Mexican avocado trees can be found both fresh
and dried in Hispanic markets or online.

Serves 6

In a large mixing bowl, combine all of the ingredients for
the papaya salsa and salt to taste, toss, and refrigerate for
at least 1 hour prior to serving.

Prepare the Sticky Coconut Jasmine Rice and keep warm.

Season the tuna with salt and pepper and dredge all sides
of the fillets in the ground avocado leaf. Heat a large skillet
over high heat. Working in 2 batches to avoid crowding,
add 1 tablespoon of the canola oil, and sear the tuna for 2
to 3 minutes per side, turning once, for rare to medium-
rare. Remove, let stand for 1 to 2 minutes, and then slice
across the grain into ¼-inch-thick slices.

Toss the arugula or watercress with the olive oil and lime
juice. Season with salt and pepper.

Spoon 1 cup of rice in the center of each plate. Arrange the
sliced tuna next to the rice, garnish with ¼ cup of the salsa
and some arugula, and serve.

PAPAYA SALSA

1 medium-size ripe red papaya, diced
(about 2 cups)
1 medium-size green papaya (optional),
diced (about 1 cup)
1 medium-size red onion, finely diced
1 habanero chile, seeded and chopped
¼ cup chopped fresh cilantro leaves
¼ cup chopped mint leaves
¼ cup extra-virgin olive oil
2 tablespoons freshly squeezed lime juice
2 tablespoons freshly squeezed orange
juice
1 tablespoon honey
Kosher salt

Sticky Coconut Jasmine Rice (page 133)

6 (6 to 7-ounce) tuna steaks, about 1-inch
thick
Kosher salt and freshly ground black
pepper
12 dried avocado leaves (see Glossary),
ground in a coffee grinder to a fine
powder
2 tablespoons canola oil

4 cups loosely packed arugula or
watercress, coarse stems removed, for
garnish
¼ cup extra-virgin olive oil
2 tablespoons freshly squeezed lime juice

HUACHINANGO YUCATECO
YUCATÁN-STYLE SNAPPER WITH ACHIOTE, WHITE RICE, AND CITRUS SALSITA

Huachinango is the name for red snapper in Mexico. This dish is a common preparation on the Caribbean coast of the Yucatán Peninsula, the most tropical region of Mexico, where you find vastly different ingredients and flavors than elsewhere in the country. The fish and rice are steamed inside banana-leaf packets and served with a tangy Citrus Salsita. This is a complete, one-dish meal. Pay attention when working with the habanero chile: It is fiery hot (see sidebar, page 6).

MARINADE

1 cup (about 4 oranges) freshly squeezed orange juice

½ cup achiote paste (see Glossary)

¼ cup (about 2 limes) freshly squeezed lime juice

¼ cup rice vinegar

2 cloves garlic

1 small yellow onion, quartered

1 bay leaf

½ teaspoon ground cumin

½ teaspoon freshly ground black pepper

¼ teaspoon ground allspice

¼ teaspoon ground cinnamon

Pinch of oregano, preferably Mexican

1 teaspoon kosher salt

½ cup canola oil

6 (6- to 7-ounce) red snapper fillets

CITRUS SALSITA

½ cup orange segments (see sidebar, page 17)

½ cup pink grapefruit segments (see sidebar, page 17)

1 small red onion, sliced in half and cut into very thin strips

1 habanero chile, seeded and finely diced

½ cup chopped fresh cilantro leaves

2 tablespoons freshly squeezed lime juice

2 tablespoons honey

continued on next page

Serves 6

MAKE THE MARINADE: In the jar of an electric blender, combine all of the marinade ingredients except the oil and purée on medium speed until smooth. With the motor running on medium speed, slowly add the oil and blend until the mixture is emulsified.

Put the fillets in a nonreactive dish, cover with two-thirds of the marinade, and refrigerate for 1 to 2 hours but no longer than 12 hours.

MAKE THE CITRUS SALSITA: In a medium-size, nonreactive bowl, gently stir all of the Citrus Salsita ingredients together. Refrigerate for at least 1 hour prior to using.

Cook the rice according to package instructions. Remove from heat and let cool.

For each fillet, cover a piece of 12 by 12-inch aluminum foil with 1 piece of banana leaf. Spoon on ½ cup of rice and add 2 slices of plantain in the center.

Lift the fillets from the marinade, allowing the excess liquid to drain back into the bowl. Season each fillet with salt and pepper, and put it on the rice and plantains. Add a few onion rings, 1 habanero ring, 2 lime slices, and 2 orange slices to each fillet and spoon 2 tablespoons of the remaining marinade over the top. Fold all four sides of the banana leaf over the top of the ingredients, fold the aluminum foil over each packet, and seal tightly.

Add 2 cups of water to a large pot with a steamer basket and bring to a simmer. Lay all six packets in the basket, seam side up, and steam for 20 minutes. Remove and let rest for 5 minutes. Open each packet, slide the banana leaf off the foil and onto a large plate, spoon on some Citrus Salsita, and serve.

½ teaspoon kosher salt

1 cup long-grain white rice

2 large fresh or frozen banana leaves, cut into 6 (12 by 12-inch) squares, or parchment paper

2 small ripe plantains, peeled and each cut on the bias into 12 slices

Kosher salt and pepper

1 small yellow onion, cut crosswise into thin rings

1 habanero chile, cut crosswise into thin rings

1 lime, cut crosswise into 12 thin slices

1 orange, cut crosswise into 12 thin slices

2 cups water

PESCADO VERACRUZANO

This is the most famous dish of the state of Veracruz, on the Gulf of Mexico. The city of Veracruz has been a busy port of call for shipping and trade for centuries, giving the region a very different and diverse cuisine, with many influences from the Mediterranean to the Caribbean. *Pescado Veracruzano* is most often prepared with Gulf fish, like snapper or rock bass, but it works well with almost any species of fish.

4 tablespoons olive oil

1 large yellow onion, diced

½ cup slivered garlic

2 cups canned whole tomatoes, drained and coarsely chopped

½ cup pitted Spanish green olives without pimentos, thinly sliced

¼ cup capers

2 tablespoons dried oregano, preferably Mexican

3 bay leaves

¼ cup dry white wine, such as sauvignon blanc or chardonnay

2 tablespoons freshly squeezed lime juice

2 tablespoons unsalted butter

Kosher salt and freshly ground black pepper

6 (6 to 7-ounce) white-fleshed fish fillets, such as bass or grouper

2 limes, cut into wedges, for garnish

Jalapeños en Escabeche (page 144) or purchased pickled jalapeños, for garnish

Serves 6

Heat a large skillet over medium-high heat. Add 2 tablespoons of the olive oil and the onion, reduce the heat to medium, and sauté until the onions are translucent, about 4 minutes. Add the garlic and continue to cook for 1 minute more. Stir in the tomatoes, olives, capers, oregano, bay leaves, and wine and gently simmer for 20 minutes. Stir in the lime juice and butter, and season to taste with salt and pepper. Pour the sauce into a warm bowl, set aside, and wash the skillet.

Preheat the oven to 400°F.

Reheat the skillet over high heat. Add the remaining 2 tablespoons of olive oil and heat until very hot. Season the fish on both sides with salt and pepper. Gently lay the fillets in the pan, taking care not to crowd the pan. If necessary, cook the fish in batches. Brown the fish on both sides, about 3 minutes per side, and transfer to the oven to bake until done, 4 to 5 minutes, depending on the thickness of the fish.

Spoon a scant ½ cup of sauce in the center of each plate, arrange the fish on top, and serve with lime wedges and *Jalapeños en Escabeche.*

DISHES FROM VERACRUZ
There are other Veracruz-style dishes in this book: Veracruz-Style Mussel Ceviche with Tomato-Lime Marinade and Spanish Olives (page 50) and Roasted Plantain Empanadas with Black Beans, Scallions, and *Queso Añejo* (page 54).

PUMPKIN SEED-CRUSTED SALMON
WITH PIPIÁN VERDE

This easy and economical dish will impress even your most discerning guests (or family members!). *Pipián Verde*, in the *mole* family, uses a simple roasted tomatillo sauce that is thickened with toasted pumpkin seeds. This recipe works great with chicken breasts, as well. Serve with the Seared Spinach with Tequila-Soaked Raisins and Spiced Pumpkin Seeds (page 138) or simply steamed asparagus for a light entrée.

Serves 6

Preheat the oven to 350°F.

Toss the pumpkin seeds in 2 tablespoons of the oil, season lightly with salt and pepper, and spread evenly on a baking sheet to lightly brown and become crisp, 5 to 7 minutes, shaking the pan occasionally. Remove the pumpkin seeds and turn the oven up to 375°F.

In the jar of an electric blender, pulse the pumpkin seeds until just coarsely ground. (Do not overblend.) Remove half of the seeds and set them aside in a flat dish or pie plate. Pour the salsa verde into the jar with the remaining seeds and purée until smooth.

Season the salmon with salt and pepper and brush the top side of each fillet lightly with egg white. Carefully press the egg-coated side into the ground pumpkin seeds.

Heat the remaining 2 tablespoons of oil in a large, oven-safe, nonstick skillet over medium-high heat until very hot. Add the fillets, crusted side down, and transfer the pan to the oven for about 3 minutes, or until the crust is lightly browned and crispy. Using a spatula or tongs, turn the fish, return the pan to the oven, and cook for 3 minutes more to cook the fish to medium. Add 1 more minute of cooking time if you prefer your fish more well done.

While the fish is cooking, in a small saucepan, heat the *Pipián Verde* sauce over medium heat until hot.

Coat each of six dinner plates with about one-third cup of the sauce, lay a fillet on top, and serve.

2 cups pumpkin seeds

4 tablespoons olive oil

Kosher salt and freshly ground black pepper

3 cups salsa verde (page 3)

6 (6 to 7-ounce) skinless salmon fillets

2 large egg whites, lightly beaten

CAMARONES AL AJILLO
JUMBO SHRIMP SAUTÉED WITH TOASTED GARLIC AND GUAJILLO CHILES

Al ajillo is a common Mexican preparation that combines the words for garlic—*ajo*—and *guajillo* chiles. These bright red chiles are very common throughout Mexico. They add a toasty, mild flavor, so the sauce is basically a decadently rich chile and garlic beurre blanc. This one-pan dish is simple and quick to make.

Serves 6

Season the shrimp with salt and pepper. Heat a large skillet over high heat. Add 1 tablespoon of the oil and quickly sear the shrimp on each side for approximately 1 minute until pink, working in batches, if necessary, to avoid steaming them. Remove the partially cooked shrimp to a plate.

Turn the heat down to medium, add the remaining tablespoon of oil and the garlic, and gently sauté until lightly browned, about 1 minute. Stir in the chiles and sauté until toasted, about 2 minutes more. Pour in the stock, raise the heat to high, and boil until the liquid is reduced by two-thirds of the original amount.

Return the shrimp to the pan, add the lime juice, and finish cooking the shrimp, about 3 minutes more. Slowly stir in the butter, waiting until each piece is incorporated before adding the next, until the sauce appears creamy. Add the cilantro and season to taste with salt. Serve over Poblano Rice with warm tortillas on the side.

36 jumbo shrimp, peeled and deveined
Kosher salt and freshly ground black pepper
2 tablespoons olive oil
8 cloves garlic, thinly sliced
4 guajillo chiles, seeded and sliced crosswise into thin strips
1 cup chicken stock
2 tablespoons freshly squeezed lime juice
6 tablespoons unsalted butter, cut into pieces, at room temperature
¼ cup chopped fresh cilantro leaves

6 cups Poblano Rice (page 129), heated
12 (6-inch) purchased flour tortillas, warmed

ANCHO-SEARED SWORDFISH
WITH GINGER–SWEET POTATO MASH, SEARED ESCAROLE, AND MANGO MOJO DE AJO

In most Hispanic recipes, *mojo de ajo* refers to a garlic butter sauce that generally includes only a touch of lime in addition to the garlic and butter. I've tweaked the sauce by adding fruit and chiles. In this version, mangoes provide a tangy-sweet addition to complement the lightly blackened swordfish. Once you have everything prepped, this dish takes just minutes to put together.

Ginger–Sweet Potato Mash (page 142)

¼ cup ancho chile powder
2 tablespoons sugar
1 teaspoon kosher salt
1 teaspoon freshly ground black pepper
6 (6- to 7-ounce) swordfish steaks, about
    1-inch thick
1 tablespoon canola oil

ESCAROLE
2 tablespoons unsalted butter, cut into
    pieces
4 cups escarole with coarse stems removed,
    cut into 2-inch pieces
Kosher salt and freshly ground black
    pepper

MANGO MOJO DE AJO
1 tablespoon canola oil
¼ cup sliced garlic
2 arbol chiles, stemmed and seeded,
    coarsely chopped or ground in a spice
    grinder
1 mango, cut into ½-inch cubes (see
    sidebar, page 149)
1 cup Lobster Stock (page 96) or chicken or
    fish stock
2 tablespoons freshly squeezed lime juice
8 tablespoons (1 stick) unsalted butter,
    sliced and softened
¼ cup chopped fresh cilantro leaves
Kosher salt

Serves 6

Prepare the Ginger–Sweet Potato Mash and keep warm.

MAKE THE SWORDFISH: Preheat the oven to 250°F.

Combine the ancho chile, sugar, salt, and pepper in a pie plate or similar flat dish. Dredge each swordfish steak individually in the chile mixture until lightly coated on all sides. Heat a large skillet over high heat, add the oil, and when it is very hot, add the swordfish steaks and sear each side for about 3 minutes, or until the fish appears "black-ened." Remove the fish to an oven-safe baking dish and transfer to the oven to finish cooking and keep warm.

MAKE THE ESCAROLE: Heat a large skillet over high heat, add the butter, and then quickly add the escarole so that the butter does not burn. Cook, turning frequently, until the escarole is wilted and hot, 2 to 3 minutes. Season to taste with salt and freshly ground pepper, cover, and keep warm over very low heat.

MAKE THE MANGO SAUCE: Heat a medium skillet over medium-high heat. Add the oil, garlic, and chiles, and sauté until lightly browned, 1 to 2 minutes. Add the mango and the stock, bring to a boil over high heat, and cook until reduced by half. Add the lime juice, gradually whisk in the butter pieces, incorporating each piece before adding the next, and continue cooking until the butter is emulsified and the sauce thickens slightly. Stir in the cilantro and season to taste with salt.

Serve a large spoonful of Ginger-Sweet Potato Mash in the center of each plate. Top with a piece of swordfish and spoon the Mango *Mojo de Ajo* over the fish. Serve the escarole on the side.

CORNMEAL-CRUSTED SOFT-SHELL CRABS
WITH PICKLED JALAPEÑO TARTAR SAUCE AND ASPARAGUS

Soft-shell crabs are a much sought after delicacy on the East Coast of the United States. Although not commonly found in Mexico, they work very well with this recipe. If soft-shells are not available, any flaky white fish, such as halibut or sole, may be used. We serve them with Pickled Jalapeño Tartar Sauce (a great marriage of North American and Mexican flavors), asparagus, and pico de gallo.

Serves 6

MAKE THE TARTAR SAUCE: Combine all of the ingredients in a small bowl and set aside.

MAKE THE CRABS: Preheat oven to 200°F.

In a medium-size bowl, mix the flour, cornmeal, chile powder, salt, and pepper. Pour the buttermilk into another medium-size bowl. Working with one crab at a time, dip each first into the buttermilk and then into the cornmeal mixture to coat evenly.

Heat a large skillet over medium-high heat. Add the canola oil and heat until hot (350°F). Slide in 3 crabs, and cook for 2 to 3 minutes per side, turning once, until golden brown and crispy. Remove with tongs or a slotted spoon and drain on paper towels. Repeat with the remaining crabs. Keep the crabs warm in the oven.

Steam the asparagus in a basket set over boiling water until bright green and crisp-tender, 5 to 6 minutes. Drain, return them to the pan with the olive oil, season with salt and pepper to taste, and shake to coat evenly. Serve 4 asparagus spears in the center of each plate with 1 crab on top. Serve the tartar sauce on the side along with some pico de gallo.

PICKLED JALAPEÑO TARTAR SAUCE

2 cups prepared mayonnaise

3 tablespoons chopped fresh oregano leaves

2 tablespoons chopped drained Jalapeños en Escabeche (page 144) or purchased pickled jalapeño chiles

1 tablespoon pickling liquid from the jalapeño chiles

1 teaspoon freshly squeezed lemon juice

Kosher salt and freshly ground black pepper

1½ cups all-purpose flour

1½ cups yellow cornmeal

2 tablespoons ancho chile powder

1 teaspoon kosher salt

1 teaspoon freshly ground black pepper

2 cups buttermilk

6 large soft-shell crabs, cleaned

1 cup canola oil

24 medium stalks asparagus, woody base snapped off

2 tablespoons extra-virgin olive oil

Kosher salt and freshly ground pepper

2 cups pico de gallo (page 2)

CAZUELA DE MARISCOS
SEAFOOD STEW WITH SMOKED CHILE BROTH

A *cazuela* is a large ceramic or cast-iron skillet in which homey, robust stews are prepared and served. This version, made with mixed shellfish and cubes of white fish in a zesty, smoky, chile-scented broth, is a perfect example. Serve it from the pot at the table along with plenty of your favorite rice and corn tortillas.

2 ancho chiles

2 dried chipotle or morita chiles, or 2 canned chipotle chiles in adobo

12 littleneck clams, scrubbed

3 cups Lobster Stock (page 96) or bottled clam broth

2 pounds whitefish fillets (such as snapper, sea bass, or halibut) cut into 1½-inch cubes

12 large shrimp, peeled and deveined

12 large scallops, side tendons removed

Kosher salt and freshly ground black pepper

¼ cup canola oil

¼ cup thinly sliced garlic

2 tablespoons freshly squeezed lime juice

2 tablespoons unsalted butter, cut into pieces, at room temperature

¼ cup chopped fresh cilantro leaves

12 (6-inch) corn tortillas, purchased or homemade (page 9), for garnish

Serves 6

Toast and rehydrate the ancho and chipotle or morita chiles (see page 6). Using a slotted spoon, transfer the chiles to the jar of an electric blender and purée, using as little of the cooking liquid as necessary to make the mixture smooth.

In a medium-size saucepan over medium heat, combine the clams and 2 cups of the stock. Cover, bring to a simmer, and cook until all the clam shells are opened, 4 to 6 minutes. Remove and reserve the clams in their shells. Discard any that do not open.

Heat a large, deep cast-iron skillet (*cazuela*) or casserole, at least 10 inches in diameter, over high heat until very hot. Season the fish, shrimp, and scallops on all sides with salt and pepper. Add 1 to 2 tablespoons of the oil, and then add the seafood to the pan. Sear on both sides until the scallops are nicely browned, about 2 minutes per side. Do this in batches, if necessary, to prevent crowding and steaming the seafood. Remove with a slotted spoon to a plate and reserve.

LEARNING TO LOVE CAZUELAS

I learned to appreciate *cazuelas* as a cooking and serving vessel at El Cardinal, a restaurant with two locations in *el centro histórico* in Mexico City. It was at their original restaurant that I had two specialties served in these cast-iron dishes. One was fresh *huitlacoche* (see Glossary) sautéed with garlic, chiles, and epazote and served with warm tortillas. The other was called *escamoles*, prepared with ant larvae, which are (believe it or not) delicious. The most intriguing part of these dishes was that they arrived at the table in their sizzling containers with the aroma strong enough to make our mouths water long before the food got to us.

In the same skillet, lower the heat to medium. Add 2 tablespoons of the oil and the garlic, and sauté until lightly browned, about 2 minutes, stirring often. Add ¼ cup of the chile purée and the remaining 1 cup of the stock, and gently boil to reduce by half, about 5 minutes.

Return all of the seafood to the pan and simmer until cooked through, 2 to 3 minutes. Stir in the lime juice and then stir in the butter a little at a time, continuously stirring until the butter is incorporated. Stir in the cilantro and season to taste with salt. Serve family style from the skillet with plenty of warm tortillas and rice on the side.

LOBSTER TUMBADA
MEXICAN-STYLE PAELLA WITH PEAS AND CARROTS

Mexican-style paella is called *tumbada*, a name that refers to the earthenware cooking and serving vessel that is often used for this dish. I use Mexican Red Rice for my *tumbada*, as well as clams, shrimp, and mussels. The dish may include any variety of fish and shellfish you choose, and it is great to serve family-style for dinner parties. Make the Lobster Stock ahead of time and reheat it before using, if you want. The remainder of the Lobster Stock may be frozen up to 3 months or used in several other recipes in this book.

3 (1-pound) lobsters

LOBSTER STOCK
Makes 12 cups
2 tablespoons light-flavored olive oil
1 large yellow onion, coarsely chopped
4 cloves garlic, coarsely chopped
2 bay leaves
1 sprig fresh thyme
½ teaspoon dried oregano, preferably
    Mexican
4 quarts water

LOBSTER-CHILE BROTH
4 cloves garlic
2 plum tomatoes
1 medium-size yellow onion
2 guajillo chiles, stemmed and seeded
2 ancho chiles, stemmed and seeded
1 canned chipotle chiles in adobo

Mexican Red Rice (page 129)

24 littleneck clams, scrubbed
24 black mussels, scrubbed
12 large shrimp, poached, peeled, and
    deveined
2 cups shelled and blanched fresh young
    peas or defrosted frozen petite peas

continued on next page

Serves 6

In a large pot, bring at least 4 quarts of salted water to a rolling boil. Add the lobsters, cover the pot, return the water to a boil, and cook the lobsters for 7 minutes more, or until the shells are bright red. Remove from the pot, wrap each lobster in aluminum foil, and let rest for at least 5 minutes.

Separate the tails from the bodies and cut them in half lengthwise through the shell from back to the front using a large chef's knife or very sharp scissors. Rinse and reserve the tail meat in the shells. Crack the claws and knuckles, remove the meat, and reserve the shells and heads. Refrigerate the lobster meat until ready to assemble the dish.

MAKE THE STOCK: Heat a large pot over medium heat. Add the olive oil and onion and sauté until the onion is translucent, about 3 minutes. Add the garlic and cook for 1 minute more. Stir in the reserved lobster shells and cook for 5 minutes more. Add the bay leaves, thyme, oregano, and water to cover. Bring the liquid just to boil and then reduce the heat and simmer gently for at least 1½ hours. Pour through a strainer into a clean pot.

MAKE THE BROTH: While the stock simmers, preheat the oven to 400°F. Put the garlic, tomatoes, and yellow onion on an oiled baking sheet and roast until the skins of the tomatoes are blistered and the onion is lightly browned and soft, 15 to 30 minutes. Remove and transfer to a medium-size pot.

Cook the guajillo and ancho chiles in a hot, dry skillet until the skins blister slightly and you can smell a toasty aroma. Transfer the chiles to the pot with the vegetables. Add the canned chipotle chiles and 6 cups of the strained lobster broth. Bring to a simmer, and then remove from the heat and let cool for 10 minutes. Working in batches, pour the broth into the jar of an electric blender and purée. Strain, pressing to extract as much liquid as possible, and reserve. Discard the solids.

Prepare the Mexican Red Rice.

Preheat the oven to 350°F.

In a large Dutch oven, casserole, or paella pan, over medium heat, combine the rice and 2 cups of warm lobster broth, and arrange the clams along with the mussels, shrimp, and lobster in a single layer on top. Heat until the liquid begins to bubble. Pour 1 more cup of lobster broth over the top, cover with a lid or aluminum foil, and transfer the pot to the oven.

After 7 minutes, lift the foil, and check that the seafood is almost cooked through and the shells have begun to open. Stir in the peas and carrots, and ladle in more stock if the rice appears to be dry. Return to the oven for 5 minutes more. Remove the pan from the oven, carefully stir in the butter, and finish by folding in the cilantro. Season to taste with salt and serve with lime wedges and plenty of warm tortillas.

2 cups peeled and finely diced carrots, blanched
3 tablespoons unsalted butter
½ cup chopped fresh cilantro leaves

2 limes, cut into wedges
12 (6-inch) corn tortillas, purchased or homemade (page 9), warmed

ROASTED CHICKEN ENCHILADAS AL PASTOR
WITH TOMATILLO SALSA VERDE AND CHIHUAHUA CHEESE

Cooking *al pastor* (see Glossary) for this recipe means using the well-known marinade from Puebla. I think this dish works especially well with boneless chicken thighs, which are far more tasty and juicy—not to mention far less expensive—than the breasts. While a true Poblano might say that this isn't authentic, it is our most popular main course. And the dish is simple to make at home. The enchiladas can be made in advance and reheated in a 350°F oven or even in a microwave oven.

3 cups Al Pastor Marinade (page 14)

3 pounds boneless, skinless chicken thighs
    or breasts

Kosher salt

SALSA VERDE

10 tomatillos, husked

1 medium-size yellow onion, quartered

6 cloves garlic

2 jalapeño or serrano chiles, stemmed
    and seeded

½ cup chopped fresh cilantro leaves

2 tablespoons freshly squeezed lime juice

Kosher salt and freshly ground black
    pepper

2 cups corn kernels, grilled and cut from
    the cob (3 or 4 ears), or defrosted high-
    quality frozen corn

1 cup chopped fresh cilantro leaves

1 cup canola oil

12 (6-inch) corn tortillas, purchased or
    homemade (page 9)

8 ounces Chihuahua cheese or Cheddar
    or Monterey Jack cheese, grated (about
    2 cups)

Serves 6

Preheat the oven to 350°F.

Put 2 cups of the prepared marinade in an oven-safe baking dish. Add the chicken, season with salt, and turn to coat. Cover with aluminum foil, and bake for 30 to 40 minutes, until cooked through.

MAKE THE SALSA: In a large saucepan, bring about 12 cups of water to a boil. Add the tomatillos, onion, garlic, and chiles, simmer for 5 minutes, and then drain. Transfer the mixture to the jar of an electric blender along with the cilantro and lime juice and purée until smooth. Season to taste with salt and pepper. Return the salsa verde to the saucepan, simmer gently for 15 minutes more, taste to adjust the seasonings, and set aside.

Lift the chicken from the marinade and discard the marinade. Let the chicken cool, and then shred the chicken and mix it with the corn kernels and cilantro. Fold in an additional 1 cup of *Al Pastor* Marinade to moisten. Leave the oven on.

Heat the oil in a medium skillet over medium-high heat until hot (350°F). Fry each tortilla for about 5 seconds on each side to soften and then drain on paper towels.

Roll about ½ cup of the chicken mixture in each tortilla, place the rolls in a 9 by 14-inch rectangular casserole, and top with grated cheese. Cover with aluminum foil and bake for 20 to 30 minutes until hot and bubbling. Serve 2 enchiladas on each plate and cover generously with salsa verde.

CAZUELA DE TINGA
ROASTED CHICKEN IN POBLANO-STYLE SWEET AND SPICY TOMATO SAUCE

This simple, traditional dish from Puebla is made with shredded chicken or pork in a smoky, chunky chile-tomato sauce that is sweetened with a bit of *piloncillo* and balanced by a touch of vinegar in the salsita. It's a great dish to prepare and serve on a cold evening or to make ahead and reheat. I use whole, cut-up chickens, but you can also use purchased rotisserie chickens. Omit the *hoja santa* if you can't find it. Be sure to serve warm tortillas.

2 (3½-pound) chickens, cut into pieces
Kosher salt and freshly ground black
    pepper
2 tablespoons olive oil
6 plum tomatoes
4 cloves garlic, peeled
1 medium-size yellow onion, quartered
2 to 4 canned chipotle chiles in adobo
2 tablespoons tomato paste
4 cups chicken stock
2 bay leaves
2 tablespoons chopped fresh hoja santa (see
    Glossary), or 1 tablespoon dried hoja
    santa (optional)
2 cups Roasted Tomato-Chipotle Salsita
    (page 20)
1 cup cubed queso fresco, for garnish
½ chopped fresh cilantro leaves, for garnish
6 cups Frijoles Borrachos (page 134)
12 (6-inch) corn tortillas, purchased or
    homemade (page 9), warmed, for
    garnish

Serves 6

Preheat the oven to 375°F.

Season the chicken with salt and pepper. Heat a large, heavy, oven-safe Dutch oven or casserole over medium-high heat. Add the oil and the chicken pieces, skin-side down, and sauté until the skin is brown and crisp, about 5 minutes. Turn the pieces over, transfer the pan to the oven, and roast until the chicken is done, about 15 minutes, or until the juices run clear when pricked deep in the thigh. Remove the pan, let the chicken cool, and then pull the meat from the bones and tear it into small shreds.

Meanwhile, roast the tomatoes, garlic, and onion on an oiled baking sheet until the skin of the tomato is lightly browned and bubbling, about 15 minutes. Transfer the vegetables to the jar of an electric blender along with the chipotles and tomato paste, and purée until smooth.

Wipe out the Dutch oven, stir in the purée, chicken stock, bay leaves, and *hoja santa* and simmer for 10 minutes over medium-low heat. Remove the bay leaves, add the Roasted Tomato-Chipotle Salsita and chicken, and heat through. Garnish with *queso fresco* and cilantro. Serve with *Frijoles Borrachos* and plenty of warm tortillas on the side.

TURKEY TOSTADA
WITH GRILLED TURKEY BREAST, FRIJOLES REFRITOS, GUACAMOLE, AND ROASTED TOMATO SALSA

Tostadas are fried corn tortillas often topped with beans, meat, tomatoes, lettuce, and salsa. They are a simple main course to enjoy for lunch or lighter dinners. When they include grilled turkey cutlets and crispy tortillas dressed with *Frijoles Refritos*, guacamole, and Roasted Tomato Salsa, they are memorable.

Serves 6

MAKE THE SALSA: Preheat the oven to 400°F. Put the tomatoes, onion, garlic, and jalapeño chiles on an oiled baking sheet, and roast them until the skins of the tomatoes are blistered and the onions are lightly browned and soft, 15 to 30 minutes, depending on your oven and the desired degree of doneness. Remove and cool completely.

Toast the arbol chiles (see page 6) and then let them cool.

Combine the roasted vegetables and the chiles with the vinegar and cilantro in the jar of an electric blender and purée until chunky-smooth.

MAKE THE TOSTADAS: Heat the oil in a medium-size skillet over medium heat until hot (about 350°F). Add the tortillas one at a time and fry until brown and crispy, 1 to 2 minutes per side, and then remove to paper towels to cool.

Heat a barbecue, gas grill, or broiler. Lightly brush both sides of the turkey cutlets with oil and season with salt. Grill or broil for 1 to 2 minutes per side, turning once, until cooked through.

Spread each tortilla with ¼ cup of *Frijoles Refritos* and 2 tablespoons of guacamole. Spoon 2 tablespoons of salsa on each tortilla and put a turkey cutlet on top.

In a bowl, mix together the oil and vinegar, add the lettuce, season with salt and pepper to taste, and toss. Spoon ½ cup of lettuce on the turkey, top with 2 tablespoons of pico de gallo and 1 tablespoon of *queso fresco,* and serve.

ROASTED TOMATO SALSA

4 plum tomatoes

1 medium-size yellow onion, quartered

4 cloves garlic

2 jalapeño chiles

2 arbol chiles

¼ cup red wine vinegar

¼ cup loosely packed fresh cilantro leaves

TOSTADAS

2 cups canola oil, for frying

6 (6-inch) corn tortillas, purchased or homemade (page 9)

1½ pounds fresh turkey breast, cut into about ¼-inch-thick slices and pounded flat into cutlets

Kosher salt

2 cups Frijoles Refritos (page 135), warmed

2 cups guacamole (page 5)

½ cup olive oil

¼ cup red wine vinegar

3 cups very thinly sliced romaine lettuce

Freshly ground black pepper

1 cup pico de gallo (page 2)

1 cup crumbled queso fresco

ANCHO-RUBBED ROASTED TURKEY
WITH MOLE POBLANO

Serve this flavorful turkey as the centerpiece for *Noche Buena* (Christmas Eve) or whenever you want a spectacularly flavorful main course. *Mole Poblano,* one of Puebla's culinary gifts to the world, is considered to be among the finest and most complex of all the *moles*. Make it on a leisurely weekend day, or if you're more ambitious, while your turkey is in the oven. Sure, it's time consuming and it makes a lot of sauce. But the results are worth every single minute. This sauce can be refrigerated for up to a week or frozen for several months and can be used on chicken or pork in addition to turkey. Warm it before serving.

MOLE POBLANO

1 pound lard (see Glossary)

10 mulato chiles, stemmed and seeded

5 pasilla chiles, stemmed and seeded

5 ancho chiles, stemmed and seeded

1 cup slivered almonds

1 cup peanuts

½ cup pumpkin seeds

½ cup sesame seeds, lightly toasted

6 cloves garlic

2 yellow onions, quartered

3 plum tomatoes

3 tomatillos, husked

1 ripe plantain, peeled and cut into 1-inch pieces

1 soft sandwich roll, cut into 1-inch cubes (about 1½ cups)

4 (6-inch) corn tortillas, purchased or homemade (page 9), cut into sixths

1 teaspoon freshly ground black pepper

1 teaspoon ground cumin

½ teaspoon ground cinnamon

½ teaspoon dried oregano, preferably Mexican

¼ teaspoon ground anise

¼ teaspoon ground allspice

1 (3-ounce) disk Mexican chocolate, finely ground

continued on next page

Serves 8 or more, depending on turkey size

MAKE THE MOLE POBLANO: Heat all but 2 tablespoons of the lard in a very large, heavy-bottomed pot over medium heat. Add the chiles in batches and fry, turning once, until the skin is blistered, 15 to 20 seconds per side. Remove with a slotted spoon or tongs to a large bowl and set aside.

In the same pot, add the almonds, cook until golden, 4 to 5 minutes, stirring occasionally, and then remove with a slotted spoon. Repeat with the peanuts and the pumpkin seeds, adding them to the bowl with the chiles.

Stir the garlic and onions into the lard and fry until the onions are soft and golden, about 5 minutes. Transfer to the bowl with the cooked ingredients. Stir in the tomatoes and tomatillos, and fry until they begin to soften and turn brown, 6 to 8 minutes. Transfer with a slotted spoon to the bowl.

Add the plantains and cook until golden, 3 to 5 minutes, and remove to the bowl. Add the bread and the tortillas, cook until lightly brown and crisp, and transfer to the bowl.

In a dry skillet, heat the pepper, cumin, cinnamon, oregano, anise, and allspice over medium heat, tossing continuously, until they smell toasty, 1 to 2 minutes, and add to the other ingredients.

Discard the remaining lard and wipe out the pot. Add the reserved 2 tablespoons of lard to the pot and heat over medium-high heat.

Combine the chocolate, sugar, raisins, and apricots with the other ingredients in a large bowl and toss together. Bring the chicken stock to a simmer. In the jar of an electric blender, add the ingredients in batches and purée, adding as little chicken stock as possible, so that the blades of the blender will turn and make a smooth paste. Scrape the mixture into the pot, and repeat with the remaining ingredients.

Fry the paste for 20 minutes, stirring continuously. Add the remaining chicken stock, bring to a simmer, and gently cook for 40 minutes more. Season to taste with salt. This sauce should have a thick, rich consistency.

MAKE THE TURKEY: Combine all of the ingredients for the rub in the jar of an electric blender and purée until smooth. Rub the turkey liberally with the mixture and roast it according to your favorite recipe. Serve with warm *Mole Poblano*.

½ cup finely chopped piloncillo or firmly
　　packed dark brown sugar
½ cup dark raisins
½ cup chopped dried apricots
3 quarts chicken stock
Kosher salt

TURKEY RUB
½ cup ancho chile powder
¼ chopped fresh thyme leaves
¼ cup chopped garlic
1 tablespoon ground avocado leaf (see
　　Glossary) (optional)
2 teaspoons dried oregano, preferably
　　Mexican
1 cup olive oil
Freshly ground black pepper

1 fresh turkey, weight of choice

ROASTED DUCK BREAST AND DUCK CARNITAS ENCHILADAS
WITH MOLE MANCHAMANTELES AND ROASTED PEACH SALSITA

Mole Manchamanteles, the fruity red *mole* from Oaxaca, is one of the more-complex and less-known *mole* sauces. The name means "tablecloth stainer," referring to its bright red color. While it does take time to prepare—so it is best made ahead of time—the results are most rewarding. In this recipe, it is the perfect partner for the duck breasts, which are cooked separately, and confit, where the combination of textures and flavors is tantalizing.

Moles are the focal point of a dish, so it is essential to serve plenty of sauce and tortillas with the duck to sop up every drop of this delectable sauce. Serve this dish with blanched green beans or sautéed greens, such as Swiss chard or mustard greens.

DUCK CARNITAS ENCHILADAS

Kosher salt

3 Long Island ducks, cut into breasts and
    leg quarters for divided use, excess fat
    and bones removed

2 pounds duck fat or lard (see Glossary)

12 black peppercorns

6 bay leaves

6 cloves garlic

6 allspice berries

2 to 3 arbol chiles

1 stick cinnamon, preferably Mexican

1 cup freshly squeezed orange juice

1 cup light Mexican beer, such as Tecate

1 cup sweetened condensed milk

1 tablespoon canola oil

Kosher salt and freshly ground pepper

1 cup golden raisins

½ cup chopped fresh cilantro leaves

1 cup canola oil, for frying

6 to 12 (6-inch) corn tortillas, purchased or
    homemade (page 9)

continued on next page

Serves 6

MAKE THE ENCHILADAS: An hour before starting the *carnitas,* liberally salt the duck legs to remove excess moisture, and set them aside in a bowl. Before cooking, blot dry.

Preheat the oven to 300°F.

In a large, oven-safe pot or baking dish with a lid, combine the duck legs, duck fat, peppercorns, bay leaves, garlic, allspice berries, chiles, cinnamon, orange juice, beer, and condensed milk, and heat on top of the stove until the fat is melted. Cover and transfer the pot to the oven for about 1½ hours, or until the duck is very tender and easily pulls away from the bone. Remove the duck legs, let them cool, and then pull off the meat from bones and shred. This is the *carnitas.* Discard the bones and skin. This can be done several hours or even a couple days ahead.

Preheat the oven to 400°F. Reheat the prepared *Mole Manchamanteles,* if cold.

Heat a large skillet over medium heat. Add 1 tablespoon of the oil and the shredded duck, and cook until lightly brown and beginning to crisp, 2 to 3 minutes. Season to taste with salt and pepper, fold in the raisins and cilantro, and reserve.

Heat a medium-size skillet over medium-low heat, add the oil, heat until hot, and quickly cook the tortillas, one at a time, for about 5 seconds per side to soften. Remove from the pan, and drain on paper towels.

Spoon ⅓ cup of duck *carnitas* in the center of each tortilla and roll it up. Put the enchiladas in an 11 by 14-inch oven-safe baking dish. Spoon 2 cups of the *mole* over the enchiladas, cover with aluminum foil, and bake in the oven for 15 to 20 minutes until heated through. Remove the cassarole, leave covered, and let stand. Reduce the oven temperature to 350°F.

MEANWHILE, MAKE THE PEACH SALSITA: Heat a medium-size, oven-safe skillet over medium heat. Add the olive oil and onion and sauté until translucent, 3 to 4 minutes. Add the garlic and serrano chiles and sauté for 1 minute more. Stir in the peaches, and continue cooking until the peaches are soft but still retain their shape, 7 to 10 minutes. Remove from the heat, let cool, and then stir in the honey and orange juice and season with about ½ teaspoon of salt or to taste. Fold in the cilantro.

MAKE THE BREASTS: Score the skin of the duck breasts diagonally through the skin, but take care not to pierce the flesh. Heat 2 very large oven-safe skillets over medium-low heat, season the duck breasts on both sides with salt and black pepper, lay them in the skillets skin side down, and sauté for 10 to 15 minutes to render off the fat and brown the skin, taking care not to burn them.

Transfer the skillets to the oven for 5 minutes to roast, turn the breasts over, and cook for 2 minutes more for medium to medium-rare. Extend the cooking time by 2 minutes, if desired, for well-cooked duck. (This may also be done sequentially, cooking two breasts in each batch.) Remove the breasts from the skillets and let them rest on a warm platter for 5 minutes.

Heat the *Mole Manchamanteles* in a saucepan over medium-high heat, stirring occasionally.

Serve one enchilada in the center of each dinner plate, and spoon on ¼ cup of *mole* sauce. Thinly slice the duck breasts crosswise and fan out the slices skin side up next to the enchilada. Garnish each plate with 2 tablespoons of the Roasted Peach Salsita and serve.

ROASTED PEACH SALSITA

3 tablespoons olive oil

1 small yellow onion, chopped

1 teaspoon chopped garlic

1 teaspoon chopped serrano chiles

3 ripe peaches, pitted and cut into medium dice, or unsweetened frozen slices

2 tablespoons honey

2 tablespoons freshly squeezed orange juice

Kosher salt

¼ cup chopped fresh cilantro leaves

4 to 5 cups Mole Manchamanteles (page 34)

MOLE

The word *mole* means "to grind or purée." This is generally done with a stone grinding wheel or in a *molcajete*. Anchos and guajillos are among the most common varieties of dried chiles available. If one or the other is unavailable, use twice the amount of one variety.

The first time I saw *Mole Manchamanteles* made in Oaxaca, I was leading a group of chefs on a culinary tour and one of our stops was El Naranjo, where the chef-owner, Iliana de la Vega, taught us to make it in her kitchen. The class started at 10 a.m. It was around 7:30 p.m. that we finally ate. We ate and drank plenty of Oaxacan mezcal until late in the evening. What lingers in my memory is the taste of that sauce made with the freshest local ingredients and freshly dried local chiles.

ARRACHERA
GRILLED MARINATED SKIRT STEAK

Grilled skirt steak, or *arrachera,* has the robust flavors of cumin, cilantro, and garlic plus some heat from the jalapeños. The cut of meat is very popular in Mexican cooking. Any steak lover will relish the flavorful grilled meat. It is important not to purée the cilantro in the marinade for too long, or it will detract from the fresh flavor and dull the bright green color. Rolling up the steak during marination helps the meat to absorb the flavors and makes it easier to store in the refrigerator. Serve with *Frijoles Borrachos* (page 134), some Roasted Tomato-Chipotle Salsita (page 20), and plenty of warm tortillas. Mexican Corn on the Cob (page 136) is another perfect addition.

¼ cup cumin seeds

1 cup olive oil

½ cup freshly squeezed lime juice

4 jalapeño chiles, cut in half lengthwise

4 cloves garlic

1½ teaspoons kosher salt

1½ teaspoons freshly ground black pepper

3 bunches cilantro, including stems

3 pounds skirt steak, trimmed and cut into 6
	serving pieces

Serves 6

Lightly toast the cumin seeds in a dry skillet over high heat until their aroma is released, 1 to 2 minutes, shaking the pan and taking care not to burn them. Combine the cumin seeds, olive oil, lime juice, jalapeño chiles, garlic, salt, and black pepper in the jar of an electric blender and purée until smooth. Scrape down the sides, add the cilantro, and pulse until just blended. Rub the meat generously with the marinade, roll the pieces up into tight logs, put them in a resealable plastic bag, and refrigerate for 24 to 48 hours, turning once or twice.

Heat a gas or charcoal grill or broiler until it is very hot. Position the rack about 4 inches from the heat. Lift the steaks from the marinade and grill each side until seared, 3 to 4 minutes, turning once. Discard the marinade. Remove to a warm platter, let rest for 5 minutes, and then transfer the steaks to a cutting board, slice across the grain into thin strips, and serve.

RUBS AND MARINADES

Rubs and marinades are frequently used in Mexican cooking not only to preserve perishable products, but also to tenderize lesser or tougher cuts of meats, like the skirt steak, or *arrachera*, used in this recipe. They also impart flavor to everything from fish and poultry to fruit. For example, what would ceviche be without its marinade? Nothing but raw—albeit very fresh—fish, or sushi. In fact, without some preseasoning, many dishes would never achieve the characteristic robust flavors that we love in modern and traditional Mexican cuisine.

GUISADO DE COSTILLAS
SHORT RIBS IN TRES CHILES BROTH

For Mexican-style comfort food, few dishes come close to fork-tender beef short ribs braised in a red chile broth made with ancho, guajillo, and arbol chiles and served over Roasted Garlic–Poblano Mashed Potatoes.

TRES CHILES SALSA

1 small yellow onion, quartered

4 cloves garlic

2 plum tomatoes

4 guajillo chiles

4 ancho chiles

2 arbol chiles

Kosher salt and freshly ground black pepper

4 pounds boneless beef short ribs, cut into 2-inch pieces

Kosher salt and freshly ground black pepper

3 tablespoons canola oil

1½ quarts high-quality chicken stock

½ teaspoon oregano, preferably Mexican

2 bay leaves

Roasted Garlic–Poblano Mashed Potatoes (page 143)

2 cups finely shredded white cabbage, for garnish

2 tablespoons freshly squeezed lime juice

4 ounces cotija or feta cheese, grated, for garnish (about 1 cup)

12 (6-inch) corn tortillas, purchased or homemade (page 9), warmed

Serves 6

Preheat the oven to 350°F.

MAKE THE TRES CHILES SALSA: Put the onion, garlic, and tomatoes on an oiled baking sheet and roast them in the oven until the skins of the tomatoes are blistered and the onions are lightly browned and soft, 15 to 20 minutes. Remove and let cool.

Toast and rehydrate the chiles in about four cups of water (see page 6). Reserve the rehydrating liquid.

In the jar of an electric blender, combine the roasted vegetables with the chiles, 2 cups of the rehydrating liquid, salt, and pepper and purée until smooth. Set aside.

Season the short ribs on all sides with salt and pepper. Heat a large, oven-safe pan on high heat. Add the canola oil and sear the short ribs on all sides until browned, about 2 minutes per side. Stir in the *Tres* Chiles Salsa and simmer for 5 minutes. Add 4 cups of the chicken stock, the oregano, and the bay leaf, and season to taste with salt and pepper. Bring the liquid to a boil, cover the pot, and transfer to the oven for 1½ hours, or until the meat is very tender, adding more stock if needed to cover the meat.

Make the Roasted Garlic–Poblano Mashed Potatoes, and keep warm.

Remove the short ribs from the cooking liquid, and strain the broth into a clean pot. Bring to a boil and reduce by a third, skimming to remove the fat from the surface. Return the short ribs to the broth and keep warm.

Toss the cabbage with the lime juice, and season to taste with salt. In each of six large, warm pasta bowls, spoon ½ cup of mashed potatoes, making a well in the center. Put 2 or 3 short ribs on top. Ladle 1 cup of the broth over the meat, garnish with ¼ cup shaved cabbage and a sprinkle of *cotija* cheese, and serve with warm tortillas.

HAMBURGER TORTA

Juicy hamburgers are an American passion. By adding guacamole and *Frijoles Refritos*, our south-of-the-border torta, or sandwich cooked on a griddle, is a *muy sabroso* lunch or light dinner similar to a panini. I like to serve this grilled sandwich with Chile Ancho–Dusted Sweet Potato Fries (page 142) and Chipotle Aioli (page 55). It's messy, but you'll love every bite.

Serves 6

Heat a griddle or large skillet over medium-high heat until hot. Season the patties on both sides with salt, pepper, and ancho chile powder. Put the patties on the griddle and cook for 3 to 4 minutes on each side for medium-rare. Remove, and if preparing them in batches, wrap them in foil to keep them warm.

Clean the griddle or skillet. Slice each roll in half and lightly butter both cut sides. Lay the buttered side down on the griddle and cook until lightly browned and toasted.

Spread the guacamole on the cut side of the top of each roll and the *Frijoles Refritos* on the bottom cut side. Put a burger on the guacamole, cover with a slice of cheese and the other half of the roll, and insert a toothpick or two to keep the sandwich together. Butter the outsides of the rolls with the remaining butter and grill both sides briefly until each torta is brown and crispy, pressing gently as they cook. Garnish with the romaine, tomato slices, onions, and sliced *Jalapeños en Escabeche*.

2½ pounds lean ground beef, formed into 6-ounce oval patties about ¾ inch thick

Kosher salt and freshly ground black pepper

2 teaspoons ancho chile powder

6 torta rolls, or soft white hoagie or sub rolls

4 tablespoons unsalted butter, at room temperature

2 cups guacamole (page 5)

2 cups Frijoles Refritos (page 135) or canned refried beans

6 romaine leaves

2 ripe tomatoes, thinly sliced crosswise

1 small red onion, thinly sliced crosswise

6 Jalapeños en Escabeche (page 144), sliced into thin strips, or jarred pickled jalapeño chiles

BARBECUED PORK TORTA

Using leftover Pork *Carnitas* (page 13), as we did in the Barbecued Pork *Sopes* with Pickled Onions (see sidebar, page 23), mix the *carnitas* with the sauce from the Chipotle-Barbecued Ribs (page 116). This makes a wonderful sandwich garnished like the Hamburger Torta but including the pickled onions from the *sope*. Serve with Ancho Chile–Dusted Sweet Potato Fries (page 142).

RIBEYE ALAMBRE
MEXICAN SHISH KEBAB

When Mexicans do kebabs, the results are full of bravado. In this version, cubes of ribeye steak are wrapped in bacon and skewered with cipollini onions, cremini mushrooms, and poblano chiles on metal *alambres*. Serve them with Arbol Chile Salsita and Pico de Gallo over *Arroz con Crema*. They're simple and delicious.

MARINADE

2 cloves garlic

1 serrano chile

¼ cup loosely packed fresh cilantro leaves

¼ cup freshly squeezed lime juice

2 tablespoons Worcestershire sauce

2 tablespoons Maggi sauce

½ teaspoon freshly ground black pepper

½ teaspoon kosher salt

½ cup olive oil

3 pounds (1½-inch-thick) ribeye steak, trimmed

Arroz con Crema (page 133)

12 strips thick-sliced smoked bacon, cut in half crosswise

continued on next page

Serves 6

MAKE THE MARINADE: In the jar of an electric blender, combine all of the marinade ingredients except the oil and purée on medium speed until smooth. With the motor running on medium speed, slowly pour in the oil and blend until smooth. Transfer the mixture to a bowl or large resealable plastic bag, add the meat, and marinate for at least 2 hours, but preferably overnight, in the refrigerator.

Prepare the *Arroz con Crema* and keep warm.

Remove the meat from the marinade and pat dry on paper towels. Discard the marinade. Heat a cast-iron or other heavy skillet over high heat. Sear the steak for 2 to 3 minutes per side, remove, and let cool. Cut it into 1½-inch cubes.

Preheat the oven to 350°F.

Cook the bacon on a baking sheet for about 7 minutes, until it is cooked but not crisp. Wrap each cube of steak with a half strip of bacon. Slide cubes of meat, onions, mushrooms, and chiles alternately onto 6 (12-inch-long) metal skewers. Refrigerate.

MAKE THE SALSITA: Stir all of the ingredients for the salsita together in a mixing bowl and set aside.

Make the pico de gallo.

Heat a barbecue, gas grill, or broiler until hot. Position the rack about 5 inches from the heat. Season each *alambre*/kebab with salt and pepper and grill for about 3 minutes per side, cooking all four sides. Transfer the *alambres* to six dinner plates. Spoon about 2 tablespoons of the salsita over the top of each one and sprinkle with 2 tablespoons of pico de gallo. Serve with warm tortillas and *Arroz con Crema*.

18 cipollini onions, blanched in boiling
    water and blotted dry
18 cremini mushrooms
4 poblano chiles, seeded and cut into ½-
    inch squares

ARBOL CHILE SALSITA
2 tablespoons chopped garlic
2 to 4 arbol chiles, stemmed and seeded,
    toasted and crushed, or 1 to 2
    tablespoons crushed red pepper flakes
¼ cup sherry vinegar
2 tablespoons Maggi sauce
2 tablespoons freshly squeezed lime juice
¼ cup chopped fresh cilantro leaves
Kosher salt and freshly ground black pepper

Pico de gallo (page 2)

CHILES EN NOGADA

Chiles en nogada are roasted poblano chiles filled with beef and pork, also known as *rellenos con picadillo*. The chiles are topped with creamy walnut sauce and fresh pomegranate seeds. This is my version of a classic dish served throughout the central regions of Mexico beginning on or near September 16, *el Día de la Independencia.* The red, white, and green colors recall the Mexican flag, *la bandera.* In Mexico, the dish is served cold or at room temperature, but we choose to serve it warm. While beef and pork are traditional, you can use all beef or even ground turkey or chicken. The most time-consuming part of this recipe is peeling the walnuts. Some stores sell them already blanched. Omit this step if you don't have time.

NOGADA SAUCE

2 cups raw walnuts or purchased blanched
   and peeled walnuts

1 cup heavy cream

1 cup crema (page 10) or sour cream

3 ounces creamy fresh goat cheese, cream
   cheese, or mascarpone (about ¾ cup)

½ cup dry sherry

2 tablespoons sherry vinegar

¼ teaspoon ground cinnamon

Pinch of nutmeg

Kosher salt

continued on next page

Serves 10

MAKE THE SAUCE: In a saucepan, cover the walnuts with water, bring to a simmer, remove from the heat, and let cool. Rinse the walnuts under cold water, peel off the brown skins, and blot dry.

In the jar of an electric blender, combine the heavy cream, crema, cheese, sherry, sherry vinegar, cinnamon, and nutmeg, and purée until smooth. Gradually add the walnuts until the sauce reaches a thick, creamy texture. Season to taste with salt, about 1½ teaspoons. If desired, strain the sauce through a fine mesh strainer for a smoother consistency. Set aside.

Roast and peel the chiles (see page 6). Set aside.

Preheat the oven to 350°F. Lightly grease a baking sheet.

Heat a large, heavy skillet over medium-high heat. Add 1 tablespoon of the oil and brown the meats in small batches. Do not crowd the pan or the meat will steam rather than brown. As the meat cooks, lift it out of the pan with a slotted spoon and transfer it to a bowl. Continue until all the meat is browned and then season to taste with salt and pepper.

Add the remaining tablespoon of oil to a large, clean skillet and heat over medium heat. Add the onion and garlic, and sauté until the onion is translucent, 3 to 4 minutes. Add the diced fruit and cook until it begins to soften, about 2 minutes.

In a small saucepan, combine the raisins and sherry, bring to a simmer, and then remove from the heat and let cool.

EL DÍA DE LA INDEPENDENCIA

The celebration of Mexico's independence from Spain in 1810 begins the night of September 15. On that evening, at city halls across the country, a reenactment of "El Grito"—when the revolutionary Father Hidalgo called for Mexican patriots to join the uprising and demand independence—is staged. On the following day, military parades march through cities and towns across the country.

Fold the meat into the onion-fruit mixture and season to taste with salt and pepper. Drain the raisins and add them along with the almonds, pine nuts, orange zest, and cinnamon to the meat mixture. Using a spoon, carefully fill each chile with about ½ cup of the filling and lay on the baking sheet. (This recipe may be done a day ahead of time to this point and refrigerated.) Bake the stuffed chiles until heated through, about 10 minutes.

This dish is commonly served family style but can also be plated. To serve, place one warm chile in the center of each plate and pour a generous amount of sauce over the center of the chile. Don't cover the entire pepper because color contrast is important. Sprinkle pomegranate seeds and parsley leaves generously over the top and serve.

10 medium-large poblano chiles
2 tablespoons canola oil
2 pounds ground beef
2 pounds ground pork
Kosher salt and freshly ground pepper
1 medium-large yellow onion, chopped (¾ cup)
4 cloves garlic, minced
1 cup peeled and diced fruit (may include apples, pears, peaches, and apricots)
½ cup raisins
1 cup dry sherry
½ cup almonds, toasted (see page 70)
½ cup pine nuts, toasted (see page 70)
2 tablespoons grated orange zest
½ teaspoon ground cinnamon
1 cup fresh pomegranate seeds, for garnish
½ cup loosely packed fresh flat-leaf parsley leaves, for garnish

LAMB BARBACOA

This slowly braised lamb is a classic for celebrations and holidays. Throughout Central Mexico, a whole goat or lamb is commonly wrapped in banana leaves and cooked in a pit in the ground. For most Americans, it is somewhat difficult to find a place to dig a pit, so this recipe is adapted for a home kitchen. While a leg or shanks may be substituted for the shoulder, the flavor is best if the meat is cooked with the bone left in.

This preparation is similar to pot roast, and like that dish, it may be served with peeled baby potatoes, carrots, and small onions (or other root vegetables), which are added to the pan about 30 minutes before the lamb is finished. Serve it in large soup bowls with tortillas and Jalapeño-Mint Salsita.

ADOBO MARINADE

6 cloves garlic

2 tomatillos, husked

1 medium-size yellow onion, coarsely chopped

2 tablespoons olive or canola oil

Kosher salt and freshly ground black pepper

6 black peppercorns

3 bay leaves

1 clove

1 star anise

1 teaspoon dried oregano, preferably Mexican

1 teaspoon cumin seeds, toasted, or ½ teaspoon ground cumin

3 ancho chiles

3 guajillo chiles

½ cup apple cider vinegar

½ cup freshly squeezed orange juice

3 or 4 large fresh banana leaves, or parchment paper

3 pounds well-trimmed and tied boneless lamb shoulder roast

2 cups beef or chicken stock

continued on next page

Serves 4 to 6

Preheat the oven to 400°F.

MAKE THE MARINADE: Toss the garlic, tomatillos, and onion with 1 tablespoon of the oil. Lightly season with salt and pepper, spread on a baking sheet, and roast until lightly browned, 20 to 25 minutes, turning occasionally.

Combine the peppercorns, bay leaves, clove, star anise, oregano, and cumin in a *molcajete* or spice grinder and grind into a fine powder.

Toast and rehydrate the ancho and guajillo chiles (see page 6). Reserve the liquid.

Combine the tomatillo mixture with the ground seasonings, chiles, vinegar, and orange juice in the jar of an electric blender, and purée until smooth, adding some of the reserved chile liquid, as needed, to make a smooth mixture. Spoon into a bowl and set aside.

Arrange the banana leaves over the bottom of a deep roasting pan or casserole, leaving enough of the leaves overhanging the pan so that you can fold them over the top to completely cover the top of the roast. Season the lamb generously with salt and pepper, put it into a large bowl, pour on the marinade, and turn to coat well. Transfer it and all of the marinade to the prepared pan. Refrigerate for at least 1 hour or overnight.

Preheat the oven to 350°F.

Before cooking, remove the meat from the refrigerator and return it to room temperature, about 45 minutes.

Pour in the stock. Fold the banana leaves over the meat, cover with aluminum foil, seal on all sides, and bake in the oven until the meat is fork tender and falling away from the bone, at least 2 hours.

MAKE THE SALSITA: Roast and then dice the jalapeño chiles (see page 6). In a medium skillet, heat the oil over medium-high heat. Add the onions, and cook until translucent, about 3 minutes. Add the jalapeño chiles, and cook for 1 minute. Stir in the vinegar, *piloncillo*, and salt and gently simmer until the mixture binds together, 8 to 10 minutes. Let cool, and then stir in the lime juice and fresh mint and set aside.

Remove the pan from the oven. Transfer the meat to a bowl and let it stand until cool enough to pull the meat from the bones. Chop or tear the lamb into medium-large shreds. Pour the cooking liquid through a fine strainer into a bowl, skim the fat from the surface, and reserve the meat and liquid.

Heat the remaining tablespoon of oil in a large skillet over medium-high heat. Add the lamb pieces and brown on all sides, 5 to 7 minutes, turning often. Ladle about 1 cup of the cooking liquid over the meat to moisten and serve family style with crumbled *queso fresco*, plenty of warm tortillas, and a couple tablespoons of Jalapeño-Mint Salsita.

JALAPEÑO-MINT SALSITA

8 jalapeño chiles
2 tablespoons canola oil
½ cup minced yellow onion
½ cup apple cider vinegar
½ cup finely chopped piloncillo or firmly packed dark brown sugar
1 teaspoon kosher salt
2 tablespoon freshly squeezed lime juice
½ cup chopped fresh mint leaves

2 cups queso fresco, for garnish
12 (6-inch) corn tortillas, purchased or homemade (page 9), warmed, for garnish

BARBACOA

Barbecuing foods in a pit is common throughout Mexico, although the ingredients vary in different parts of the country. Most famously, this technique is used in the Yucatán to prepare *Cochinita Pibil*, or baby pig that is marinated in achiote and citrus juices and then roasted in banana leaves. The pork is traditionally served with a pot of soup made from pigs' inner organs.

In Oaxaca, lamb cooked in this manner for several hours becomes meltingly tender and moist, with a slightly smoky flavor. The lamb is placed on steaming mats woven from palm leaves with layers of anise-scented *hoja santa* (see Glossary) leaves below. The meat is typically served with *blandas*,

the huge, handmade corn tortillas typical of the region. The idea is to pile the *blanda* with lamb and some of the salsa or *mole negro* that is served at every table.

In central Mexico, *maguey* leaves from a certain agave or cactus plant are baked until limp and used to wrap meats for the pit barbecue to impart a distinct flavor. In the north, they prefer to barbecue a kid goat for *cabrito al pastor*. Maguey hearts are also used to make mezcal and tequila.

This flavorful style of cooking was originally developed by indigenous people who didn't have ovens. Today, it has been adapted for modern ovens all over Mexico.

CHIPOTLE-BARBECUED RIBS

This dish was created by my friend and former Dos Caminos chef Ivy Stark. These succulent ribs are roasted in banana leaves, like *barbacoa* (see sidebar, page 115), but then they are grilled and brushed with Chipotle Barbecue Sauce. We commonly serve these ribs with Black Bean and Chorizo Chile (page 81) and Jicama Slaw (page 20). You can generally find frozen banana leaves at Asian or Hispanic markets.

PORK RIB RUB

¾ cup freshly squeezed orange juice

¼ cup achiote paste (see Glossary)

3 shallots, sliced

2 lemons, thinly sliced

2 limes, thinly sliced

2 bay leaves, crumbled

2 tablespoons chopped fresh thyme leaves

2 tablespoons chopped fresh oregano

2 tablespoons chopped fresh rosemary

1 tablespoon minced fresh garlic

1 teaspoon ground cumin

1 teaspoon ground coriander

4 to 5 pounds pork spare ribs or baby back ribs

Kosher salt and freshly ground black pepper

3 or 4 large fresh banana leaves or parchment paper

continued on next page

Serves 6

In a large bowl, mix all of the rub ingredients together. Season the ribs on both sides with salt and pepper and cover them evenly on both sides with the rub mixture.

Preheat the oven to 350°F. Line a deep roasting pan with a piece of aluminum foil that is long enough to fold the ends over the ribs once the pan is filled. Arrange the banana leaves over the top of the foil, leaving enough of the leaves overhanging the pan so that you can fold them over on top to completely cover the top of the ribs.

Lay the ribs on the banana leaves, spoon on the remaining rub, including the sliced lemons and limes, and fold the leaves over the ribs to cover. Cover the pan with aluminum foil and seal tightly. Bake for 2½ to 3 hours, or until the meat is tender and falling off the bones. Remove the pan from the oven, partially uncover, and allow the ribs to cool to room temperature. Once cooled, scrape off the excess rub and cut the slabs into 2- to 3-rib sections. Refrigerate the ribs if you are not grilling them immediately.

MAKE THE SAUCE: Combine all of the ingredients for the barbecue sauce in a saucepan, bring to a simmer over medium heat, cook for 5 minutes, and then remove and let cool.

Remove the ribs from the refrigerator and return to room temperature. (If the ribs are cooked directly from the refrigerator, they may take longer to cook.) Light a charcoal or gas grill and position the rack about 4 inches from the heat. Or turn on a broiler and position the rack so that the ribs do not touch the heat. Leave the broiler door slightly ajar while cooking.

Lay the ribs, meat side down, on the grill and spoon on
some sauce. Cook until the sauce begins to caramelize
and the meat begins to get crispy with little brown spots,
about 1 minute. Turn, baste the ribs, and continue cooking
for 1 minute more. Turn the ribs, cooking twice on each
side, 4 to 6 minutes total cooking time, basting each time
with a brush, and being careful not to burn the sauce. After
three coats on each side, the ribs are ready to serve.

CHIPOTLE BARBECUE SAUCE

12 ounces ketchup

3 canned chipotle chiles in adobo, finely
  chopped

¼ cup molasses

¼ cup Worcestershire sauce

¼ cup honey

¼ cup rice vinegar

2 tablespoons Dijon mustard

1 cup chicken stock

COCHINITA PIBIL
SLOW-ROASTED ACHIOTE-MARINATED PORK WITH HABANERO-PICKLED ONIONS

This very traditional dish comes from the Yucatán, where whole pigs are marinated, wrapped in banana leaves, and cooked for long hours in a wood-fired outdoor pit. Banana leaves add a highly aromatic flavor to this dish, but if they are not available, simply use aluminum foil. At Dos Caminos, we use whole suckling pigs, but a boneless pork shoulder works wonderfully well at home. Needless to say, it is difficult to find a pit on Park Avenue, in New York City, but at the restaurant, we improvise. The fresh banana leaves and achiote provide the important authentic taste.

MARINADE

1 cup freshly squeezed orange juice

½ cup achiote paste (see Glossary)

¼ cup freshly squeezed lime juice

¼ cup rice vinegar

2 cloves garlic

1 small yellow onion, quartered

1 bay leaf

1 teaspoon kosher salt

½ teaspoon ground cumin

½ teaspoon freshly ground black pepper

¼ teaspoon ground allspice

¼ teaspoon ground cinnamon

Pinch of oregano, preferably Mexican

½ cup canola oil

3 pounds boneless pork shoulder, well trimmed and cut into 2½-inch cubes

Kosher salt and freshly ground black pepper

1 medium-size yellow onion, quartered

6 cloves garlic, coarsely chopped

1 Valencia or Navel orange, cut into crosswise slices

4 sprigs oregano

1 habanero chile, cut in half lengthwise

continued on next page

Serves 6 generously

MAKE THE MARINADE: In the jar of an electric blender, combine all of the marinade ingredients except the canola oil, and purée on medium speed until smooth. With the blender running on medium speed, slowly pour in the canola oil and blend until emulsified.

Season the pork on all sides with salt and pepper. In a large mixing bowl, toss the pork with the onion, garlic, orange, oregano, and chile. Add the marinade and mix well. Cover and refrigerate for 1 hour.

MAKE THE PICKLED ONIONS: Combine all of the ingredients for the pickled onions in a medium-size, nonreactive saucepan and bring to a boil over medium heat. Remove the pan from the heat and refrigerate for at least 1 hour or preferably overnight prior to using.

Remove the marinated pork from the refrigerator and stir in the chicken stock.

Preheat the oven to 350°F. Line a 9 by 13-inch covered casserole with a sheet of aluminum foil that's long enough to fold the ends over the pork once the dish is filled. Repeat with the banana leaves.

Scrape all of the ingredients into the casserole, fold the leaves and foil over the meat, crimping the foil to seal. Transfer the pot to the oven and bake until the meat is fork tender, 1½ to 2 hours.

Prepare the Sautéed Sweet Plantains with Fresh Crema and Sea Salt.

Using a slotted spoon or tongs, transfer the pork to a deep serving bowl or platter, tent with foil, and keep warm.

Pour the cooking liquid through a fine strainer into a medium-size saucepan and bring to a boil over medium-high heat, skimming off the fat as it rises to the surface. Season the broth to taste with salt and pepper. Serve the dish family style with the Sauteéd Sweet Plantains and the garnishes on the side. Ladle some broth over each serving and pass the remainder.

HABANERO-PICKLED ONIONS
2 large yellow onions, thinly sliced
1 small beet, peeled and quartered
1 habanero chile, cut in half
1 cup apple cider vinegar
1 cup water
2 bay leaves
1 teaspoon kosher salt

2 cups chicken stock
4 to 6 whole banana leaves, fresh or frozen, or parchment paper

Sautéed Sweet Plantains with Fresh Crema and Sea Salt (page 145)

12 (6-inch) corn tortillas, purchased or homemade (page 9), warmed, for garnish
4 ounces cotija or feta cheese, grated, for garnish (about 1 cup)

BANANA LEAVES

Besides being used to line barbecue pits in Oaxaca, banana leaves are used to wrap tamales because they make the packets impervious to the liquid in which they are cooked.

TAMARIND PASTE

Tamarind paste is made from the tamarind fruit, originally from North Africa and Asia. The paste has a sharp, acidic taste with a hint of sweetness that is reminiscent of lemon juice. It is often used in Middle Eastern and East Indian dishes as part of a glaze for meats and poultry, in curry sauces, and even desserts. Look for it in Middle Eastern, Asian, and Hispanic markets.

CHIPOTLE AND TAMARIND-GLAZED PORK CHOPS
WITH APPLE PICO DE GALLO

Pico de gallo, or "rooster's beak," is a familiar condiment traditionally made with raw tomatoes. Here, crisp apples are used instead of the tomatoes, making a worthy topping for juicy pork chops with an apple cider–tamarind glaze. These chops are also a natural with Beer-Battered Onion Rings (page 137) and Mexican Corn on the Cob (page 136).

Serves 4

MAKE THE GLAZE: In a small saucepan, combine all of the glaze ingredients and simmer for 5 minutes until well blended and smooth. Scrape into the jar of an electric blender and purée until smooth. Set aside.

MAKE THE APPLE PICO DE GALLO: Combine the apples and lime juice. Stir in the onion, chile, and cilantro, and season to taste with salt.

Position the rack of a gas barbecue, grill, or broiler about 5 inches from the heat and heat until hot. Lightly brush the pork chops with oil, season with salt and pepper, and grill them for 3 minutes on each side, turning once. Brush liberally with the glaze and continue cooking each side for 1 to 2 minutes more for a total of 10 minutes, or until pink in the middle. Remove to a platter or serving plates, top with the Apple Pico de Gallo, and serve.

GLAZE

1 cup unfiltered apple cider
1 cup tamarind paste
¼ cup apple cider vinegar
2 tablespoons honey
2 canned chipotle chiles in adobo
1 teaspoon yellow mustard seeds
Kosher salt

APPLE PICO DE GALLO

4 Granny Smith apples, peeled and cut into medium cubes
2 tablespoons freshly squeezed lime juice
1 small red onion, cut in half lengthwise and thinly sliced
1 jalapeno or serrano chile, thinly sliced
¼ cup chopped fresh cilantro leaves
Kosher salt

4 (1½-inch-thick) loin pork chops
1 tablespoon olive oil
Freshly ground black pepper

PILONCILLO AND CANELA-GLAZED HAM

Fresh ham is, in my humble opinion, one of the most flavorful and forgiving cuts of pork there is. It is great freshly cooked, reheated, or served cold. I enjoy this Mexican twist on the classic baked ham during the Easter holiday festivities with a simple potato gratin layered with roasted poblano peppers and *cotija* cheese.

1 (8- to 10-pound) bone-in, shank-end fresh ham, skin removed, and trimmed of all but a ½-inch layer of exterior fat
Kosher salt and freshly ground black pepper
1 pound piloncillo, chopped, or dark brown sugar
4 sticks cinnamon, preferably Mexican canela
2 cups freshly squeezed orange juice, or more as needed
2 cups apple cider vinegar, or more as needed
2 jalapeño chiles, thinly sliced
5 star anises
3 cloves
2 bay leaves

Serves 10

Preheat the oven to 450°F.

With a sharp knife, score the fat of the ham in a diamond pattern and rub generously with salt and pepper.

In a medium saucepan, mix together the *piloncillo*, cinnamon, 2 cups of the orange juice, 2 cups of the vinegar, jalapeño chiles, star anises, cloves, and bay leaves and bring to a boil over high heat. Lower the heat to a simmer and cook until the *piloncillo* is completely dissolved and the glaze is slightly reduced.

Set the ham on a rack in a roasting pan, fat side up, and roast for 20 minutes. Reduce the temperature to 325°F, baste with half of the glaze, and continue roasting. Occasionally baste the ham with the remaining glaze and with the pan juices until a meat thermometer inserted into the thickest part of the ham registers 155°F, 3½ to 4 hours. If the pan juices begin to dry up, add a little water to the bottom of the pan. If the top of the ham browns too much, cover it loosely with lightly greased aluminum foil.

Remove from the oven and let the ham stand, loosely tented with foil, for 30 to 40 minutes, during which time the internal temperature will rise. Carve the ham into thin slices and serve.

GREEN MARKET VEGETABLE QUESADILLAS

Vegetarians, as well as anyone who wants a tasty dish, can enjoy these grilled quesadillas filled with vegetables and cheese as an entrée or an appetizer. A light green salad works well as an accompaniment.

Serves 6

Make the pico de gallo and set aside.

Heat a gas grill or barbecue. In a large mixing bowl, toss the sliced vegetables and chiles with the olive oil, salt, and pepper, and grill until nicely marked and tender, about 2 minutes per side, turning once. Remove with metal tongs.

Lay 6 tortillas on a flat surface and spread ¼ cup of the cheese evenly over each one. Layer a variety of grilled vegetables on top of the cheese, sprinkle ¼ cup of the remaining cheese on top of the vegetables, add 2 tablespoons of Roasted Tomato Salsa, and cover with the remaining tortillas, pressing to secure the ingredients in place.

Heat a griddle or large skillet over medium heat. Spread about 1 teaspoon of butter on each side of the quesadillas and griddle them, like a grilled cheese sandwich, until brown and crispy. Cut each quesadilla into 4 pieces, like a pizza, and garnish with pico de gallo and crema

Pico de gallo (page 2)

QUESADILLAS
3 small zucchini, cut on the bias into ¼-inch-thick slices
3 small yellow squash, cut on the bias into ¼-inch-thick slices
2 chayotes (see Glossary), cut into ¼-inch-thick slices
1 medium-size red onion, cut into ½-inch slices
2 poblano chiles, sliced in half lengthwise and seeded
¼ cup olive oil
Kosher salt and freshly ground black pepper
12 (6-inch) purchased flour tortillas
2 pounds Chihuahua or white Cheddar cheese, grated (about 8 cups)
1 cup Roasted Tomato Salsa (page 101)
4 tablespoons unsalted butter
½ cup crema (page 10) or sour cream, for garnish

TAMAL DE CAZUELA CON VERDURAS
TAMALE AND GRILLED-VEGETABLE CASSEROLE

This is such a satisfying casserole, I urge you to try it, even though the list of ingredients looks long. Use the vegetables I suggest or your own mixture. The casserole can also be prepared one day ahead and then cooked when ready.

GUAJILLO CHILE SALSA

4 plum tomatoes

4 guajillo chiles, stemmed and seeded

2 tablespoons canola oil

1 small yellow onion, cut into 1-inch cubes

2 tablespoons chopped garlic

¼ cup chopped piloncillo or firmly packed
    dark brown sugar

¼ cup freshly squeezed orange juice

¼ cup apple cider vinegar

1 cup water

½ cup heavy cream

Tamale dough (masa) (page 9)

¼ cup olive oil

1 medium-size red onion, cut into ½-inch
    slices

1 poblano chile, cut in half lengthwise,
    seeds and membranes removed

1 red bell pepper, cut in half lengthwise,
    seeds and membranes removed

4 large portobello mushrooms, stemmed

1 small zucchini, cut into ½-inch slices

1 small Japanese eggplant, cut into ½-inch
    slices

Kosher salt and freshly ground black
    pepper

¾ cup fresh corn kernels (about 1 ear) or
    defrosted high-quality frozen corn

1 teaspoon canola oil (optional)

continued on next page

Serves 6 to 8

Preheat the oven to 400°F.

MAKE THE SALSA: Put the tomatoes on an oiled baking sheet and roast them until the skins of the tomatoes are blistered, 15 to 20 minutes. Remove them, let cool, and coarsely chop.

Cook the guajillo chiles in a hot, dry skillet until the skins blister slightly and you can smell a toasty aroma. Let them cool and then cut into 1-inch cubes.

Heat a medium-size saucepan over medium heat. Add the canola oil and onion and sauté until lightly browned, about 3 minutes. Add the garlic, sauté for 1 minute, and then stir in the guajillo chiles, *piloncillo*, and chopped tomatoes, and sauté for 3 minutes more. Add the orange juice, vinegar, and water and simmer gently for 15 minutes. Stir in the heavy cream and simmer for 5 minutes more. Pour the salsa into the jar of an electric blender and purée until smooth. Set aside.

Prepare the tamale dough (*masa*).

Heat a barbecue grill or broiler.

In a large bowl, combine the olive oil with all of the vegetables except the corn and season to taste with salt and pepper. Put the corn on the grill and cook until the kernels are lightly browned and tender, 4 to 5 minutes. Remove, let cool, and then cut off the kernels. Or heat a small skillet over medium-high heat, add the canola oil and corn, and quickly sauté the kernels until lightly toasted, 4 to 5 minutes, shaking the pan occasionally.

Working in batches, grill the other vegetables until cooked through and beginning to soften. Let them cool and then cut them into ½-inch cubes. Combine the vegetables with the toasted corn, cilantro, and thyme and adjust the seasonings to taste.

Preheat the oven to 325°F. Butter the bottom of a 9 by 13-inch casserole dish and spread a ¾-inch layer of *masa* evenly on the bottom.

Spoon a generous layer of Guajillo Chile Salsa over the *masa*, spread the grilled vegetables on top, cover with aluminum foil, and bake for 30 minutes.

Raise the temperature to 375°F, remove the foil, sprinkle both cheeses over the top, and return to the oven for 10 to 15 minutes more, until cheese is lightly browned and melted. Let the casserole rest for 5 minutes. Serve warm with the remaining Guajillo Chile Salsa and garnish with the pico de gallo and crema.

¼ cup chopped fresh cilantro leaves

1 tablespoon chopped fresh thyme

6 ounces Chihuahua, Monterey Jack, or Cheddar cheese, grated, for garnish (about 1½ cups)

2 ounces queso fresco, crumbled, for garnish (about ½ cup)

½ cup pico de gallo (page 2), for garnish

½ cup crema (page 10) or sour cream, for garnish

ACOMPAÑAMIENTOS

Chapter Five: SIDE DISHES

RICE, BEANS, AND CORN—the most significant staples

in the Mexican diet—appear with nearly every meal served there. Often thought to be boring or an afterthought on the plate, these foods can become something far more exciting in the right hands. My Mexican friends have shown me this again and again when I visit, and I've tried to rejuvenate our versions to be equally compelling and diverse. There are six different rice recipes alone in this chapter, from the most familiar Mexican Red Rice to *Arroz con Crema*, a creamy rice blended with cheese, roasted corn, and chiles.

I am a big fan of beans because they are both delicious and high in protein. The menu at Dos Caminos, like those at most Mexican restaurants, includes refried beans. Sadly, at many restaurants, the beans are often bland and overused. My recipe for *Frijoles Refritos* will erase any bad rap beans have in this country! I also include my favorite beans, *Frijoles Borrachos*, stewed with chiles and beer. They are great with Lamb *Barbacoa*.

This chapter also includes a tasty array of squash, mushroom, and other vegetable side dishes. Most of our entrée recipes suggest complementary side dishes to accompany them. However, be creative: Mix and match them to suit your own palate. Side dishes in Mexico are often served family style in the center of the table. Remember, the most important, almost essential, side dish is always plenty of warm tortillas.

MEXICAN RED RICE

Red rice is a staple in Mexican cooking. Diced, blanched carrots and peas are sometimes added to the dish for color and taste.

Serves 6

Preheat the oven to 375°F.

Heat a medium-size, oven-safe saucepan over medium heat. Add the canola oil, butter, and onion, and sweat the onion until it is translucent, 3 to 4 minutes. Stir in the tomato paste and cook for 1 minute more. Add the rice and sauté until the grains begin to lightly color.

Add the tomato juice, water, serrano chiles, bay leaves, and salt. Bring to a simmer. Cover the dish and transfer to the oven. Bake for 20 minutes. Remove the pan from the oven, let it stand for 5 minutes, remove the bay leaves and the chiles, fluff with a fork, taste to adjust the seasonings, and serve warm.

1 tablespoon canola oil
1 tablespoon unsalted butter
¼ cup finely diced yellow onion
2 tablespoons tomato paste
2 cups long-grain white rice
2 cups tomato juice
2 cups water
2 serrano chiles, cut in half lengthwise
2 bay leaves
1 teaspoon kosher salt

POBLANO RICE

A flavorful rice to serve with *Camarones al Ajillo* (page 91) as well as with steak or chicken dishes.

Serves 6

Seed and roast the chiles (see page 6) and then cut them into ½-inch cubes.

While the chiles are cooking, bring the water and salt to a boil in a medium-size saucepan. Stir in the rice, cover, lower the heat, and simmer until the rice is tender, about 20 minutes.

Meanwhile, heat a medium-size skillet over medium-high heat until hot. Add the oil and corn and cook until the kernels are lightly brown, shaking the pan occasionally, 3 to 4 minutes. Set aside. Once the rice is done, stir in the epazote, chiles, corn, and cheese, and serve.

3 to 4 poblano chiles
4 cups water
1½ teaspoons kosher salt
2 cups long-grain white rice
2 teaspoons olive oil
2 ears fresh corn, or 1½ cups high-quality defrosted frozen corn kernels
½ cup chopped fresh epazote or cilantro leaves
½ cup shredded cotija cheese

ARROZ VERDE
GREEN RICE

Puréed spinach and cilantro add a beautiful green hue and zesty taste to boiled rice, taking it far beyond a mundane side dish.

3 poblano chiles
3 tablespoons canola oil
1½ cups diced yellow onion
1 teaspoon chopped garlic
2 cups long-grain white rice
4 cups warm water
2 cups firmly packed spinach leaves
2 cups firmly packed fresh cilantro leaves
Kosher salt and freshly ground black
    pepper

Serves 6

Roast and peel the poblano chiles (page 6). Set aside.

Heat a medium-size pot over medium-high heat, add the oil, onion, and garlic and sauté until the onion is translucent. Add the rice and cook for 2 minutes more. Add the water and bring to a rapid boil over high heat. Lower the heat, cover, and cook for 20 minutes, or until all the water is absorbed and the rice is cooked. Remove the pan from the heat and let the rice cool.

Meanwhile, in a large pot, cover the spinach and cilantro with water. Bring just to a boil and then drain and shock the spinach and cilantro under cold water. Working with a handful at a time, squeeze out the excess water.

In the jar of an electric blender, combine the spinach, cilantro, and poblanos and purée until smooth. In a bowl, blend the rice with the spinach purée and season to taste with salt and pepper. In a saucepan, heat the rice over medium heat, stirring frequently, and serve.

SAFFRON PAELLA RICE

Saffron and turmeric impart a vibrant color and flavor to our paella rice. This creamy-toothsome rice dish is essentially a risotto. Throughout Mexico, you'll find dishes that are similar to this, but most often they are made with long-grain white rice. To further embellish the dish, you might add a cup of finely diced chorizo that is first sautéed in a little oil and drained before being stirred into the cooked rice.

4 tablespoons unsalted butter

¾ cup diced yellow onion

1 teaspoon chopped garlic

2 cups short-grain rice (such as Arborio or Valencia)

5 to 6 cups Lobster Stock (page 96) or high-quality chicken stock

2 pinches of saffron

1 tablespoon ground turmeric

Kosher salt and freshly ground black pepper

Serves 6

In a medium-size pan, melt 2 tablespoons of the butter over medium-high heat. Add the onion and cook until translucent, about 5 minutes. Stir in the garlic, cook for 1 minute, and then add the rice, stirring to coat it thoroughly with the butter. Cook for 3 to 4 minutes, or until the grains look opaque.

Meanwhile, in a separate pan, combine the stock with the saffron and turmeric and bring to a boil.

Begin adding the heated stock to the rice slowly—about½ cup at a time—so that the rice stays wet but is never completely covered with liquid. Once the rice absorbs the entire first amount of liquid, add another ½ cup, stirring constantly. Continue cooking, adding liquid and stirring, until the grains of rice are tender, with a tiny, firm spot at the center of each grain, 17 to 19 minutes of simmering time. Stir in the remaining butter, season to taste with salt and pepper, and serve.

ARROZ CON CREMA
CREAMY RICE WITH ROASTED CORN AND POBLANO CHILES

This creamy, tasty side dish is a willing partner for all grilled and broiled meat, poultry, and fish dishes. Chihuahua cheese comes from the Mexican state of the same name.

Serves 6

Roast the poblano chiles (see page 6), and then cut them into small cubes.

Heat a griddle or gas grill until hot. Cook the corn until the kernels are lightly browned and tender, turning the ears to cook all sides. Remove the ears, let them cool, and then cut off the kernels. If using frozen corn, lightly cover the bottom of a skillet with oil and heat over medium-high heat until hot. Add the corn kernels and quickly sauté until lightly toasted, shaking the pan occasionally.

In a medium-size saucepan over medium heat, combine the rice, cream, corn, and poblano chiles and simmer until the mixture is hot and binds together, 3 to 5 minutes, stirring frequently. Add the cheeses and stir until creamy. Stir in the cilantro, season to taste with salt, and serve warm.

2 to 3 poblano chiles
2 ears fresh corn, or 1½ cups defrosted
  high-quality frozen corn
4 cups cooked long-grain white rice
1 cup heavy cream
2 ounces Chihuahua or Monterey Jack
  cheese, grated (about ½ cup)
1 ounce cotija or feta cheese, grated (about
  ¼ cup)
¼ cup chopped fresh cilantro leaves
Kosher salt

STICKY COCONUT JASMINE RICE

The tropical flavor of coconut is an ideal complement for Avocado Leaf–Crusted Tuna with Spicy Papaya Salsa (page 85) or any poultry dish.

Serves 6

Wash the rice in several changes of cold water to remove the excess starch.

In a medium saucepan, combine the rice, coconut milk, water, cinnamon, sugar, and salt. Cover, bring to a gentle simmer, and cook for 20 minutes. Remove from the heat and let stand for 10 minutes. Fluff the rice gently with a fork, taste to adjust the seasonings, and serve.

2 cups jasmine rice
3 cups coconut milk
1 cup water
1 stick cinnamon, preferably Mexican
2 tablespoons sugar
1 teaspoon kosher salt

FRIJOLES BORRACHOS
DRUNKEN BEANS

Frijoles borrachos are the ideal accompaniment for skirt steak, ribs, or barbecued chicken. The beans are called "drunken" because they are simmered in beer. They are also known as *frijoles charros,* or "cowboy beans," and are best when prepared a day in advance and reheated.

1 tablespoon olive oil

4 strips smoked bacon, chopped

1 medium-size yellow onion, chopped

2 cloves garlic, chopped

2 ribs celery, finely chopped

1 large carrot, finely chopped

2 tablespoons tomato paste

2 tablespoons Dijon mustard

2 canned chipotle chiles in adobo, chopped

¼ teaspoon dried oregano, preferably Mexican

¼ teaspoon chopped fresh thyme leaves

4 cups cooked pinto beans or rinsed and drained canned beans

1 cup light Mexican beer, such as Tecate

Kosher salt

Serves 6 to 8

Heat a 4-quart saucepan over medium heat. Add the olive oil and bacon and cook until the bacon begins to brown and become crisp. Add the onion and sauté until it is translucent, 3 to 4 minutes. Stir in the garlic, celery, and carrot and cook for 3 minutes more.

Stir in the tomato paste, mustard, chipotles, oregano, and thyme. Add the pinto beans and beer and enough water to cover (about 2 cups). Season with salt, bring to a simmer, cook for 20 minutes, and then remove from the heat and let cool.

MEXICAN COWBOYS

There is a long tradition of cowboys and ranchers in the north of Mexico. Thus, you find dishes that are called "cowboy style," such as these beans, *Huevos Rancheros* (page 174), and *Arrachera* (page 104). My family did have horses while I was growing up, but I was never a cowboy and actually preferred to ride motorcycles.

FRIJOLES REFRITOS
REFRIED BEANS

A quintessential basic of Mexican cooking, *Frijoles Refritos* are often served with melted cheese on top. Either black beans or pinto beans are commonly used.

Serves 4 to 6

In a large skillet, heat the lard or shortening over medium heat. When hot, stir in the onion, sauté slowly until lightly caramelized, 6 to 9 minutes, and then stir in the beans. Mash the beans with a potato masher or the back of a large spoon, adding small amounts of the reserved cooking liquid (or water), as needed, until the mixture is smooth. Season to taste with salt. Sprinkle with cheese and serve.

2 tablespoons lard (see Glossary), solid vegetable shortening, or canola oil

1 medium-size yellow onion, diced

2 cups cooked black beans or pinto beans, cooking liquid reserved, or rinsed and drained canned beans

Kosher salt

2 ounce cotija or feta cheese, grated (about ½ cup)

MUSHROOMS
SAUTÉED WITH GARLIC, CHILES, AND FRESH EPAZOTE

These are great as a side dish or when served on top of a grilled steak or roast chicken. Or use the mushrooms scrambled with your eggs. Epazote is an herb that tastes like a cross between mint, basil, and oregano. Mexicans often use it in egg dishes. If you can't find epazote, use oregano.

Serves 6

In a large skillet over medium heat, combine the oil, shallots, and garlic and sauté until the shallots are limp, 2 to 3 minutes. Stir in the arbol and serrano chiles and sauté for 1 minute more to release the chile flavor. Turn the heat up to medium-high, add the mushrooms, and cook until lightly browned and tender, 5 to 7 minutes. Add the lime juice and epazote, season to taste with salt and pepper and serve.

2 tablespoons olive oil

2 tablespoons finely chopped shallots or red onion

2 cloves garlic, chopped

1 to 2 arbol chiles, stemmed and seeded, coarsely chopped

1 serrano or jalapeño chile, coarsely chopped

3 cups cremini or white mushrooms, quartered

1 tablespoon freshly squeezed lime juice

¼ cup chopped fresh epazote (see Glossary)

Kosher salt and freshly ground black pepper

MEXICAN CORN ON THE COB

A delectable side dish for lovers of fresh corn on the cob. It is commonly served from carts on the streets in Mexico. The cart vendors also offer several garnishes, including mayonnaise, lime juice, cheese, and chile powder.

Kosher salt
6 ears corn, shucked
1 cup Chipotle Aioli (page 55)
4 ounces cotija or feta cheese, grated
    (about 1 cup)
2 tablespoons ancho chile powder
1 lime, cut into 6 wedges

Serves 6

Bring a large pot of salted water to a boil over high heat. Add the corn and boil over high heat for 5 to 7 minutes, until the corn is cooked. Remove and drain.

Heat a barbecue, gas grill, or broiler until hot. Brown the corn on all sides, and then remove the ears from the grill, and spread with a generous amount of Chipotle Aioli. Sprinkle with *cotija* cheese and ancho chile powder. Serve with lime wedges on the side.

CORN ESQUITES

Mexicans simply love fresh corn, either on or off the cob. In *esquites*, sautéed corn kernels are traditionally seasoned with epazote (see Glossary) and chiles and served as a soupy side dish. It's a great way to showcase sweet fresh corn.

Serves 8

With a sharp knife, cut the corn kernels off the cobs. Heat a large skillet over medium-high heat. Add the butter, onion, and serrano chiles and cook for about 1 minute. Stir in the corn and cook until the corn has softened, about 5 minutes. Stir in the chicken stock, add the epazote, and season to taste with salt.

Scrape the mixture into a large bowl. Stir in the mayonnaise, cheese, and lemon juice. Ladle the corn into individual bowls or cups and serve.

7 ears fresh corn, or 4 cups defrosted high-quality frozen corn

2 tablespoons unsalted butter

¼ cup diced yellow onion

4 serrano chiles, cut into small dice

½ cup chicken stock

2 tablespoons chopped fresh epazote (see Glossary)

Kosher salt

¼ cup prepared mayonnaise

1 ounce cotija or feta cheese, grated (about ¼ cup)

1 tablespoon lemon juice

BEER-BATTERED ONION RINGS

The beer in the batter—preferably a light Mexican brand like Tecate—makes these onion rings crunchy and simply addictive.

Serves 6

In a large bowl, combine all of the dry ingredients. Add the beer and mix until all the lumps are gone.

In a deep fat fryer or deep skillet, heat the oil to 350°F. Preheat the oven to 200°F.

Dip the onion rings individually into the batter, letting the excess fall back into the bowl, and gently drop them into the hot oil. Fry until golden brown, remove with tongs to paper towels to drain, transfer to a baking sheet, and keep warm in the oven until all the onion rings are fried.

2 cups all-purpose flour

1 teaspoon baking powder

1 teaspoon chile powder

1 teaspoon kosher salt

Freshly ground black pepper

1 (12-ounce) can light Mexican beer, such as Tecate

3 to 4 cups canola oil, for deep frying

2 large yellow onions, cut into ½-inch thick slices and separated into rings

SEARED SPINACH
WITH TEQUILA-SOAKED RAISINS AND SPICED PUMPKIN SEEDS

Serve this uniquely appealing spinach dish with shrimp, meat, or fish entrées. With the exception of the final cooking, all of the steps may be done several hours in advance. *Reposado* tequila has aged for 2 months in oak barrels. Soaking raisins in tequila plumps and moistens them. The combination of the nutty toasted pumpkin seeds with the fruity-sweetness of the raisins gives a big hit of flavor to the spinach.

½ cup golden raisins
¼ cup reposado tequila (see page 197)
1 pound baby spinach leaves
2 tablespoons unsalted butter
½ cup Spiced Pumpkin Seeds (page 51)
Kosher salt and freshly ground black
    pepper

Serves 6

In a small saucepan over high heat, combine the raisins with the tequila and enough water to cover. Bring to a boil, remove from the heat, and let cool. Drain and discard the liquid.

Fill a 5-quart pot with water, add about 2 tablespoons of salt, and bring to a boil.

While the water is heating, fill a large bowl three-quarters full with half ice and half cold water. Set the bowl near the boiling water.

Add the spinach to boiling the water in batches and blanch for 10 to 15 seconds, or until wilted. With a slotted spoon or strainer, quickly remove the spinach from the boiling water to the ice bath to stop the cooking and help set the bright green color. Drain the cooled spinach in a colander and squeeze out the excess moisture with your hands. If not assembling the dish right away, refrigerate the spinach in a colander.

Heat a large skillet over medium-high heat. Add the butter, and then add the spinach, Spiced Pumpkin Seeds, and raisins, and quickly sauté until heated through. Season to taste with salt and pepper. Drain any excess liquid and serve family style on a warm plate.

ROASTED BUTTERNUT SQUASH HASH
WITH POBLANO PEPPERS

This colorful, tasty side dish can easily be made several hours ahead and reheated. Warm it up in a large skillet over medium-high heat.

2 tablespoons unsalted butter
2 pounds butternut squash, peeled, seeded, and cut into ½-inch cubes
2 red bell peppers
2 poblano chiles
4 strips thick-cut bacon, cut crosswise into ½-inch pieces
1 small yellow onion, cut into ¼-inch cubes
1 tablespoon freshly squeezed lime juice
Kosher salt and freshly ground black pepper
¼ cup loosely packed fresh epazote (see Glossary), cut crosswise in thin strips

Serves 6

Preheat the oven to 400°F.

Melt the butter in a large skillet over medium heat. Add the squash, turn to coat with butter, scrape onto a large baking sheet, and roast in the oven until golden and tender, about 15 minutes, turning occasionally.

Meanwhile, roast and peel the red bell pepper and poblano chiles (see page 6). Cut into ¼-inch pieces and set aside.

Heat the skillet over medium-high heat, add the bacon, and cook until brown and crisp. Remove with a slotted spoon to paper towels and drain. In the same skillet, over medium-high heat, add the onion and sauté until pale golden color, 3 to 4 minutes. Add the roasted peppers, squash, and cooked bacon and toss to blend. Stir in the lime juice, season to taste with salt and pepper, and stir in the epazote.

SAVORY SWEET POTATO FLAN

Silky flans are an elegant accompaniment for the Roasted Duck Breast with *Mole Man-chamanteles* (page 104). Use them in place of the duck *carnitas* enchilades or as a side with any fall meat dish.

Serves 6

Preheat the oven to 375°F.

Roast the potatoes for 45 minutes, and then cool, peel, and mash them until smooth. Using a handheld electric mixer, blend in all of the remaining ingredients until smooth.

Butter 6 (6-ounce) custard cups or ramekins or a 2-quart round baking dish.

Reduce the oven heat to 325°F. Bring a kettle of water to a boil. Ladle the flan mixture into the ramekins or baking dish.

Put the ramekins or pan in another larger pan and transfer both to the oven. Pour in boiling water to come about two-thirds of the way up the sides of the ramekins or pan and cover with aluminum foil. Bake for 20 minutes, or until the center is firm to the touch and springs back when gently pressed with a finger. (If using a larger baking dish, cook for 35 to 40 minutes.) Remove the pan and carefully lift off the foil. Let the flans rest in the water for 10 minutes and then run a thin-bladed knife around the edge of each ramekin, invert onto plates, and serve warm. Serve the larger flan from the baking dish.

2 pounds jumbo red yams or sweet potatoes
4 large eggs, beaten
1 cup heavy cream
2 tablespoons honey
1 tablespoon ancho chile powder
1 teaspoon ground cumin
1 tablespoon freshly squeezed lime juice
Kosher salt and freshly ground black pepper

GINGER-SWEET POTATO MASH

These pleasantly spiced yams or sweet potatoes have a refreshing acidic flavor note that enlivens the taste, thanks to the touch of fresh lime juice. Although I prefer jumbo red yams because of their dark orange flesh and great firm texture, I refer to this dish as "sweet potato mash" because people are more familiar with sweet potatoes. Either potato works in this dish.

3 large red yams or sweet potatoes
2 tablespoons unsalted butter
2 tablespoons freshly squeezed lime juice
1 teaspoon freshly grated ginger
1 teaspoon ancho chile powder
Kosher salt

Serves 6

Preheat the oven to 375°F.

Bake the yams on a baking sheet for 45 minutes, or until cooked through and soft. Cool for a few minutes and then carefully peel them while still warm. Put the yams into a medium-large saucepan pan over low heat and mash with a fork until chunky-smooth. Stir in the butter, lime juice, ginger, chile powder, and 1 teaspoon of salt or to taste. Serve warm.

ANCHO CHILE-DUSTED SWEET POTATO FRIES

Fried sweet potatoes (or sweeter tasting red yams) are our favorite version of fries. Zesty ancho chile powder sprinkled on before serving pops up the taste.

3 very large red yams or sweet potatoes,
    peeled and cut into ¼-inch sticks
4 cups canola oil, for frying
2 teaspoons ancho chile powder
Kosher salt
1 lime, cut into wedges

Serves 4 to 6

Preheat the oven to 350°F.

In a large bowl, toss the yam pieces with 2 tablespoons of the canola oil. Lay them in a single layer on a baking sheet and bake for about 10 minutes to partially cook. Remove the pan and let cool.

Heat the remaining oil in a 4-quart saucepan over medium heat (325°F). Add the yam pieces to the pan in batches and fry for a few minutes, or until they are brown and crispy, watching that they do not burn. Remove with a slotted spoon and drain on paper towels. Transfer them to a large bowl, toss with the chile powder, season to taste with salt, and serve with wedges of lime.

ROASTED GARLIC–POBLANO MASHED POTATOES

Serve these vibrant green mashed potatoes with grilled fish, *Mole Poblano*, or any time you want a colorful and tasty side dish.

Serves 6

In a large pot, cover the potatoes with water, add 1 tablespoon of salt, bring the water to a boil, and cook the potatoes until just tender when pierced with a knife, 10 to 12 minutes. Remove the pot from the heat and set aside the potatoes to cool in the water.

While the potatoes are cooking, roast the poblano chiles over high heat, directly on a gas burner, over an open flame, or under the broiler, until the skins begin to blister and turn black. Use tongs to turn the chiles to char them all over, even on the ends. Transfer the chiles to a bowl, cover them tightly with plastic wrap until cooled, and then scrape off the skin with a paring knife. Cut in half lengthwise and remove the seeds and membranes.

Preheat the oven to 350°F. Roast the garlic on an oiled baking sheet pan until soft, about 10 minutes.

Heat the cream and butter in a small pan over medium heat until the butter melts. Remove and let cool slightly. In the jar of an electric blender, combine the cream and butter with the scallions, cilantro, spinach, and poblano chiles and purée until smooth.

Drain the potatoes in a colander, allowing a few minutes for all of the water to drain off, and then transfer them to a large pot set over medium heat. Mash the potatoes with a potato masher or a fork until smooth (or chunky-smooth, according to your own taste), and then gradually fold in the purée mixture and salt to taste. Serve warm.

4 large russet or other baking potatoes, peeled and quartered
2 large Yukon Gold or other yellow potatoes, peeled and quartered
Kosher salt
2 poblano chiles
4 cloves garlic
¾ cup heavy cream
4 tablespoons unsalted butter
½ cup chopped scallions
½ cup loosely packed fresh cilantro leaves
½ cup chopped fresh spinach leaves

ROASTED PLANTAIN MASH

Plantains are very popular in Mexican cuisine. They are used both green (unripe) and when the skin has blackened and the fruit is soft. As with bananas, their cousins, the riper the plantain is, the sweeter it tastes. This sweet side dish is a good counterpart to spicy hot dishes.

4 very ripe plantains
¼ cup crema (page 10) or sour cream
2 tablespoons unsalted butter
1 tablespoon honey
Kosher salt

Serves 6

Preheat the oven to 400°F.

Put the unpeeled plantains on a baking sheet and cook for 25 to 30 minutes, or until the skin turns very black and begins to bubble. Remove, let the plantains cool enough to handle, and then peel and transfer them to a large saucepan. Using a fork, mash the plantains until they are creamy but still chunky. Fold in the crema, butter, and honey. Season to taste with salt and serve warm.

JALAPEÑOS EN ESCABECHE
PICKLED JALAPEÑOS

Pickled jalapeños are a terrific condiment to embolden everything from basic torta sandwiches to grilled chicken. It will keep in the refrigerator for up to a month when stored in a tightly sealed container.

12 large jalapeño chiles, cut in half
    lengthwise
6 cloves garlic
2 medium carrots, thinly sliced
1 large yellow onion, thinly sliced
10 whole black peppercorns
4 bay leaves
2 tablespoons kosher salt
½ teaspoon oregano, preferably Mexican
3 cups apple cider vinegar
3 cups water

Makes 1½ quarts

In a large, nonreactive saucepan, combine all of the ingredients and bring to a simmer. Cook for 3 minutes, remove the pan from the heat, and let cool. Transfer to a clean glass or plastic container, cover, and refrigerate.

MEXICAN BREAKFAST POTATOES

Serve these crunchy, flavorful potatoes with *Chorizo con Huevos* (page 177) and all of the other breakfast dishes in this book, or as a side dish with chicken or steak. They can be reheated in an uncovered dish.

Serves 6

Roast the chiles and bell peppers (see page 6). Slice them into thin strips and set aside.

In a large, heavy, oven-safe skillet over medium heat, cook the bacon until crisp and separated into pieces. Remove the bacon from the pan and blot on paper towels, leaving the rendered bacon fat in the pan.

In a large pot, combine the potatoes and water to cover. Add about 1 tablespoon of salt and bring to a boil. Boil the potatoes until they are just cooked through, about 10 minutes, or until a knife inserted in the middle goes in and slides out easily. Immediately drain the potatoes in a colander, and rinse with cold water to stop the cooking. Blot dry with paper towels.

Preheat the oven to 400°F.

Reheat the skillet with the bacon fat over medium-high heat, add the oil and onion, and sauté until lightly browned, 6 to 8 minutes. Stir in the potatoes and all of the remaining ingredients, season to taste with salt and pepper, and bake in the oven until crispy and brown, stirring occasionally, about 15 minutes. Remove and serve warm.

2 poblano chiles
2 red bell peppers
6 thick-cut slices of bacon, cut into
　　½-inch pieces
2 pounds baby yellow or red potatoes,
　　scrubbed and cut into wedges
Kosher salt
2 tablespoons olive oil
1 large yellow onion, cut in half lengthwise
　　and sliced into thin strips
2 cloves garlic, chopped
1 tablespoon ancho chile powder
1 teaspoon ground cumin
Pinch of dried oregano, preferably Mexican
Freshly ground black pepper

SAUTÉED SWEET PLANTAINS
WITH CREMA AND SEA SALT

A traditional accompaniment for *mole* dishes but also delicious with *Cochinita Pibil* (page 118).

2 tablespoons unsalted butter
2 to 3 large, very ripe plantains, peeled and
　　cut into ½-inch slices
½ cup crema (page 10) or sour cream
Coarse sea salt

Serves 6

Heat a large skillet over medium heat. Add the butter and plantains and cook slowly until the plantains are lightly browned on both sides, about 2 minutes per side, turning once. Serve hot on a serving platter with the crema drizzled on top and sprinkled with coarse salt.

POSTRES Y DULCES

Chapter Six: PASTRIES AND SWEETS

LIKE AMERICANS, MEXICANS LOVE

sweets of all sorts. Mexican desserts are quite different from ours—and they often tend to be very sweet—so I work with our talented pastry chef, Hugo Reyes, to interpret traditional sweets so they satisfy the tastes of our customers but stay true to their original flavor.

Hugo combines the classical pastry background he gained from working with some of New York's best pastry chefs with memories from his childhood in Puebla, Mexico, and adds some playful modern interpretations. One good example of this is the classic *cajeta*, which is a goat's milk *dulce de leche* sauce, a variation of which is used on my favorite, *Crepas de Cajeta* (Roasted Banana Crepes). This sauce has recently become a phenomenon here, with everything from ice cream to coffee borrowing the complex caramel flavors. Similarly, the addition of bananas and chocolate add a updated twist to the traditional and much-loved Chocolate Banana *Pastel de Tres Leches*.

Since the cocoa plant is indigenous to Mexico, we focus a lot of attention on chocolate, which has been used for centuries in both sweet and savory dishes there. For our desserts at the restaurant, we often combine Oaxacan and European styles of chocolate to produce a richer, creamier texture along with the very unique Mexican flavor.

In this chapter, I have included our versions of favorite Mexican classics like flan, along with Buñuelos and the doughnutlike *Churros*. For me, desserts should be irresistible but also retain the spirit of Mexico.

TEQUILA-FLAMBÉED TROPICAL FRUITS
WITH VANILLA ICE CREAM

A quick but refreshing and festive finale to any meal. This is my Mexican take on Bananas Foster, a much-loved dessert that originated in New Orleans.

Serves 6

Heat a large skillet over medium heat. Stir together the butter and brown sugar and cook until a smooth syrup forms. Add the bananas, mangoes, pineapple, and lime juice to the syrup and cook, spooning the syrup over the fruit, for 1 minute. Remove the pan from the heat and carefully pour in the tequila. Return the pan to the heat and carefully ignite the liquid. Swirl the pan until the flames die out.

In each of six dessert bowls, serve a large scoop of vanilla ice cream. Spoon on the fruit and pour on the sauce.

4 tablespoons unsalted butter

1 cup firmly packed dark brown sugar

4 firm, ripe bananas, peeled and diced

2 mangoes, peeled and diced

1 pineapple, peeled, cored, and diced

1 tablespoon freshly squeezed lime juice

¼ cup premium añejo tequila (see sidebar, page 197)

Vanilla ice cream

TO CUT A MANGO

Mangoes are a very popular fruit in Mexico. Once you realize how the interior pit is situated, it is simple to cut them up in the most efficient way.

First figure out which is the flat side of the mango—that is the wide side of the large seed inside. Cut a thin slice from one end of the mango. Stand the mango on this flat base, and cut off one side of the mango as close to the seed as possible. Turn and cut off the other side along the seed. You will still have the skin on the mango and a small horizontal strip of unpeeled flesh on both sides next to the pit. Using a spoon, scoop out the flesh and cut it into small cubes. You should have about 4 cups of chopped mango.

CHURROS
MEXICAN DOUGHNUTS

Crunchy, fried strips of dough, or *churros*, originated many years ago in Spain. Spaniards brought them to Mexico and Argentina. They can be made in several shapes, but Mexicans prefer them in long, fluted strips. *Churros* are eaten for breakfast with a cup of thick *Champurrado* (page 191) or served with Oaxacan Chocolate Fondue (page 160). Warning: They're irresistible!

Makes 12 to 15 (8- to 10-inch) pieces

In a medium-size pan with a heavy bottom, combine the water, butter, ¼ cup of the sugar, ¼ cup of the oil, 1 teaspoon of the cinnamon, the salt, and vanilla and bring to a boil. Stir in the both flours and cook over medium heat for about 10 minutes, stirring constantly with a wooden spoon, until the dough no longer sticks to the sides and forms a ball in the center of the pan.

Transfer the hot mixture to a large bowl. Using a handheld electric mixer, beat in the eggs, one at a time, until fully incorporated. Let the dough cool and then spoon it into a pastry bag fitted with a large star tip.

Line a baking sheet with parchment. Pipe the batter in 10-inch strips onto the parchment, and let them set for 8 to 10 minutes, or until firm but slightly tacky to the touch.

In a large skillet, heat the remaining oil over high heat to 325°F. Slide the strips of dough into the pan one at a time and fry until golden brown, 5 to 7 minutes, turning once. Remove from the pan with a slotted spoon to paper towels to drain. Combine the remaining sugar and cinnamon. Toss the *churros* in the cinnamon-sugar to coat and then serve warm.

2½ cups water
8 tablespoons (1 stick) unsalted butter
¼ cup sugar, plus ½ cup for coating
¼ cup canola oil, plus 4 cups for frying
1 teaspoon ground cinnamon, plus 1 teaspoon for coating
1 teaspoon kosher salt
½ teaspoon vanilla extract
2 cups cake flour
½ cup all-purpose flour
3 large eggs

COCONUT FLAN
WITH TROPICAL FRUIT SALSITA

Rich baked egg custard is one of the most classic of all Mexican desserts. Traditionally, flan is vanilla scented, but we simply love it flavored with caramel, toasted coconut, and coconut milk. The creamy, smooth textures and tastes marry perfectly with the sweet salsita.

1 cup sugar

3 tablespoons water

1½ cups canned coconut milk

1 (4-ounce) can evaporated milk

1 (4-ounce) can sweetened condensed milk

4 large eggs

2 large egg yolks

½ cup sweetened shredded coconut,
    for garnish

continued on next page

Serves 8

Lightly coat 8 (4-ounce) custard cups or ramekins or 1 (8-inch) round cake pan with vegetable spray. Preheat the oven to 325°F. Bring a kettle of water to a boil.

Put the sugar in a small, heavy-bottomed saucepan and add just enough water to wet the sugar. Cook over medium-high heat, swirling the pan constantly, until the sugar turns a rich amber color, about 10 minutes. Immediately pour about 1 to 2 tablespoons of the caramel into the bottoms of each cup, or pour all of the caramel into the round cake pan, rotating to cover evenly.

In a large bowl, using a handheld mixer or whisk, blend the coconut milk with the evaporated and condensed milks. Add the eggs and yolks, and continue to mix until well blended. Pour the mixture through a fine strainer into a bowl and then ladle it into the prepared custard cups or pan. Put the ramekins or pan into another larger pan and transfer both to the oven. Pour in boiling water to come about two-thirds of the way up the side of the ramekins or pan and cover with aluminum foil. Bake for 20 to 25 minutes, or until the flan is firm at the edges and wiggles slightly in the center, or 35 to 40 minutes for the larger single flan.

Remove the pan from the oven, remove the foil, and let the pan sit at room temperature until the water cools. Remove the custard cups or cake pan and refrigerate for at least 2 hours. The flan can prepared up to this point up to a day ahead.

After you remove the flan from the oven, raise the oven temperature to 350°F and toast the coconut on a baking sheet, stirring frequently, for about 10 minutes, or until lightly browned.

MAKE THE SALSITA: In a small saucepan, combine the mango, papaya, pineapple, orange, sugar, and orange juice and bring to a boil over high heat. Turn the heat down to low and reduce until about one-third of the liquid has evaporated. Remove the salsita from the pan, cool completely, and then stir in the mint.

To release the flan from the ramekins or cake pan, trace around the edges with a sharp, thin-bladed knife to loosen. Invert the ramekins onto individual dessert plates, or the cake pan onto a large dessert platter, gently tapping on the bottom of the pan if necessary. Cut the large flan into wedges. To serve, spoon the salsita around each serving of flan and garnish with the toasted coconut.

TROPICAL FRUIT SALSITA

1 cup diced mango (see sidebar, page 149)

1 cup diced papaya

1 cup diced pineapple

1 cup fresh orange segments (see sidebar, page 17)

½ cup sugar

¼ cup freshly squeezed orange juice

¼ cup finely shredded fresh mint leaves

BUÑUELOS

These puffed, crispy, golden fritters are a staple at Christmastime and at every carnival throughout Mexico. I like them drizzled with vanilla-infused honey and cinnamon sugar.

Serves 8

In a bowl, sift together the flour, 2 tablespoons of the sugar, the baking powder, and the salt. Add the eggs, milk, lard or shortening, and butter and mix to form a ball. Turn the dough out on a lightly floured board and knead until smooth, adding more flour or milk by the tablespoon, as needed. Cut the dough into four equal pieces, cover each with plastic wrap, and refrigerate for at least 30 minutes.

Cut the vanilla bean in half lengthwise, scraping out all of the seeds from the center of the pod, and combine the pod and seeds with the honey in a small saucepan. Warm over low heat to about 165°F, and let the mixture steep while making the *buñuelos*.

In a small bowl, combine the remaining ½ cup of the sugar with the cinnamon. Take the dough out of the refrigerator. Cut each piece of dough into 12 equal pieces, and roll them into balls. On a floured board, flatten each ball into a disk about ¼ inch thick and then press your thumb into the center of each disk to form a well.

In a large, deep skillet, add enough oil to measure at least 1½ inches deep. Heat the oil to 350°F. Add the *buñuelos* in batches and fry until golden brown, turning once. Remove from the pan with a slotted spoon and drain on paper towels. Remove the vanilla bean from the honey. Quickly toss the *buñuelos* in the cinnamon-sugar, drizzle with the warm honey, and serve hot.

3 cups all-purpose flour, sifted

2 tablespoons sugar, plus ½ cup for coating

½ teaspoon baking powder

1 teaspoon kosher salt

2 large eggs, beaten

¼ cup milk

3 tablespoons lard (see Glossary) or solid vegetable shortening

3 tablespoons unsalted butter, softened

1 vanilla bean or 1 teaspoon vanilla extract, to drizzle

1 cup honey

1 teaspoon cinnamon

4 cups canola oil, for frying

PUMPKIN FLAN
WITH WARM GINGERBREAD AND APPLE SALSITA

For Thanksgiving (even though it's not a Mexican holiday) or any autumn celebration, this dessert will satisfy diners from children to adults. This combination of silky pumpkin flan, lightly spiced apple salsita, and gingerbread is a perfect dessert for *El Día de los Muertos*. For a simpler version, use purchased gingerbread, or omit it.

1½ cups sugar

2 tablespoons water

1½ cups canned or fresh pumpkin purée

1 cup sweetened condensed milk

1 cup evaporated milk

1 cup milk

½ teaspoon ground cinnamon

¼ teaspoon ground nutmeg

¼ teaspoon ground ginger

5 large eggs

APPLE SALSITA

2 Granny Smith apples, peeled, cored, and
   diced

½ cup golden raisins

½ cup dark rum

½ cup sugar

1 stick cinnamon, preferably Mexican

1 star anise

continued on next page

Serves 8

Lightly coat 8 (4-ounce) oven-safe ramekins or 1 (9-inch) round cake pan with vegetable spray. In a small skillet, combine 1 cup of the sugar with the water and bring to a boil over medium-high heat. Cook, swirling constantly, until the sugar melts and turns golden brown, about 10 minutes. Immediately remove the pan from the heat and pour the caramel into the prepared dishes, rotating the cups or pan to evenly coat the bottom.

Preheat the oven to 325°F. Bring a kettle of water to a boil.

In a large bowl, whisk the remaining ½ cup of sugar into the pumpkin purée. Add the condensed, evaporated, and whole milks along with the cinnamon, nutmeg, ginger, and eggs and blend until smooth. Pour the mixture into the caramel-lined ramekins or cake pan.

Put the ramekins or pan into another larger pan (or two pans, if needed) and transfer them to the oven. Pour in boiling water to come about two-thirds of the way up the side of the ramekins or pan and cover with aluminum foil. Bake for 20 to 25 minutes (or 40 minutes for a single, large flan). Carefully remove the pan, and lift off the foil. Check that the flan is firm at the edges and jiggles a little in the center. If not, return the pan to the oven and bake about 5 minutes more (5 to 10 minutes for the larger version), or until the flans are done. Remove the pan and let the flans cool in the water. Leave the oven on.

MAKE THE APPLE SALSITA: In a medium-size skillet over medium heat, combine all of the Apple Salsita ingredients, bring to a simmer, and cook until the liquid is reduced to a syrup and the apples are tender, 5 to 6 minutes. Spoon into a bowl and refrigerate. Before serving, remove the cinnamon and star anise.

MAKE THE GINGERBREAD: Butter and flour an 8-inch square cake pan.

In a small bowl, stir the molasses and hot water together until blended. In a large bowl, combine the dry ingredients and the butter and stir until smooth. Slowly add to the molasses, stir until blended, and then beat in the egg. Spoon the batter into the prepared pan and bake for 15 to 20 minutes, or until the center bounces back when gently pressed with a finger.

Remove the pan from the oven and set it on a rack until cool enough to handle. Using a sharp paring knife, cut around the edges of the pan to loosen the cake, invert, remove the cake, and cut it into squares.

To release the flan from the ramekins or cake pan, trace around the edges with a sharp, thin-bladed knife to loosen. Invert the ramekins onto individual dessert plates, or the cake pan onto a large dessert platter, gently tapping on the bottom of the pan if necessary. Serve warm with gingerbread and spoonfuls of Apple Salsita.

GINGERBREAD

½ cup dark molasses
½ cup hot water
1½ cups all-purpose flour
½ cup finely chopped piloncillo or firmly packed dark brown sugar
½ teaspoon baking soda
½ teaspoon ground ginger
½ teaspoon ground cinnamon
½ teaspoon kosher salt
8 tablespoons (1 stick) unsalted butter
1 large egg, beaten

CREPAS DE CAJETA
ROASTED BANANA CREPES

These warm, roasted banana–filled pistachio *crepas* are topped with a very traditional, thick *cajeta*—a caramel-like *dulce de leche* made from goat's milk. While cow's milk may be substituted, the goat's milk adds a distinctive tang to the sauce. *Cajeta* may be made ahead of time and refrigerated for up to six months in the refrigerator in an airtight jar. Using two flours gives the crepes a more delicate texture, but all-purpose flour alone may also be used. The texture of the crepes is best if the batter is chilled overnight. At the minimum, it should chill for an hour. The best way to grind pistachios is in a clean coffee grinder. Otherwise, finely chop them.

CREPAS

1 cup cake flour

1 cup all-purpose flour

½ cup sugar

¼ cup finely ground pistachios

½ teaspoon kosher salt

2 large eggs plus 1 egg yolk

¾ cup whole milk

4 tablespoons unsalted butter, melted

1 tablespoon brandy

CAJETA

8 cups goat's milk or whole cow's milk

1½ cups sugar

1 tablespoon vanilla extract

CANDIED PISTACHIOS

1 cup shelled pistachio nuts

1 egg white

2 tablespoons sugar

8 tablespoons (1 stick) unsalted butter

1 cup firmly packed light brown sugar

1 teaspoon ground cinnamon

1 teaspoon vanilla extract

6 firm ripe bananas

Serves 6

MAKE THE CREPAS: In a large bowl, mix together both flours, ½ cup of the sugar, the ground pistachios, and the salt. Beat the 2 whole eggs and 1 egg yolk together until smooth, and whisk them into the dry ingredients. In a small saucepan, heat the milk, butter, and brandy until warm. Whisk them into the flour mixture until well combined and chill for at least 1 hour.

MAKE THE CAJETA: In a medium-size saucepan, combine the milk, 1½ cups of sugar, and vanilla. Cook the *cajeta* over medium-low heat until it turns a golden caramel color and the 8 cups are reduced to 2 cups, at least 2 hours, stirring occasionally. It will be fairly thick, like condensed milk.

MAKE THE CANDIED PISTACHIOS: Preheat the oven or to 350°F. Line a baking sheet with parchment paper. In a large bowl, combine the pistachios with the egg white, tossing to coat evenly. Sprinkle on the sugar, turning to coat the pistachios evenly, and then spoon them into a single layer on the baking sheet. Bake for 10 minutes, turning the nuts occasionally, until they are dry and nicely caramelized. Remove and let cool.

Spray an 8-inch nonstick skillet with nonstick cooking spray, and heat over medium-high heat. Ladle ¼ cup of the *crepa* batter into the pan, rotating it so that the batter covers the bottom evenly with a very thin coating. Cook for 1 minute, or until tiny brown spots form on the bottom of

the *crepa*. Using your fingers or a spatula, lift the *crepa* at the edge, flip it over, and cook the second side for 1 minute more, or until just done. Remove from the pan to a flat plate and set aside. Cover the cooked *crepas* with a second plate as they are done.

Melt the butter in a large skillet over medium heat. Stir in the brown sugar, cinnamon, and vanilla. Reduce the heat to low and cook until the sugar is dissolved. Raise the heat to high and boil, stirring occasionally, until the sauce is a pale golden color and syrupy. Peel the bananas and cut into ½-inch slices. Add them to the pan and cook for 3 to 4 minutes over medium heat to warm, turning occasionally. Let them cool for 10 minutes. With a slotted spoon, divide the bananas among the *crepas*. Fold into triangles (as shown) or roll up as you would a traditional crepe. Serve on a dessert plate with some *cajeta* sauce spooned on top and the candied pistachios sprinkled on top.

CAJETA

What is known as *dulce de leche* in Spain and other Spanish-speaking countries is called *cajeta* in Mexico. This sauce, made with slowly caramelized milk and sugar, has recently become popular in the United States. It is delicious on *Churros* (page 151) or on ice cream.

Cajeta is characteristically made with goat's milk or a combination of goat and cow's milk.

Celaya, Guanajuato, has been Mexico's *cajeta* capital since early Spaniards first brought the sweet sauce to the New World. Goats were used because they were so plentiful in the region. *Cajeta* has always been packed in a small wooden box, or *cajete*, from which the sauce takes its name.

APPLE AND SWEET CHEESE EMPANADAS

If you thought empanadas were only savories, this heavenly apple-and-cheese-filled variation will correct that misconception. There are many sweet empanadas throughout Mexico and Latin America. Most of them contain fruits such as bananas or pineapple. For example, in the town of Xico, in Veracruz, they prepare a giant empanada filled with roasted bananas that I think is awesome.

Serves 6

In a large, heavy skillet, melt the butter over medium-high heat. Add the apples, ½ cup of the sugar, ½ teaspoon of the cinnamon, the salt, and the dark and golden raisins and cook until the apples are caramelized and soft, 5 to 7 minutes, stirring occasionally. Remove from the heat and cool.

In a large bowl, using a handheld mixer, beat the cream cheese on low speed until soft. Add another ½ cup of sugar and ½ teaspoon of cinnamon and mix just to incorporate. Add the mascarpone and mix just to blend. (Do not overmix.) When the apple mixture is cool, fold it into the cream cheese mixture and chill for 30 minutes.

Preheat the oven to 375°F. Line a baking sheet with parchment paper.

Dust a flat workspace with flour. Using a lightly floured rolling pin, roll out the puff pastry to a thickness of ¼ inch. Using a plate or a cardboard template measuring 5 inches in diameter and a sharp paring knife, cut out six pastry circles. Brush each of the disks lightly with the egg wash, spoon ¼ cup of the filling in each center, fold in half, and seal by pressing with the tines of a fork perpendicular to the edge.

Lay the empanadas on the baking sheet. Combine the remaining ¼ cup of sugar and ¼ teaspoon cinnamon in a small bowl. Brush the empanadas with the egg wash and sprinkle a little cinnamon-sugar on top. Bake in the center of the oven for 8 minutes, turn the pan back to front, and bake for 8 minutes more, or until the empanadas are a light golden color. Remove from the oven and transfer to a rack to cool. Sprinkle the empanadas with a little confectioners' sugar and serve with a scoop of vanilla ice cream.

3 tablespoons unsalted butter

3 Gala apples, peeled, cored, and cut into chunks

1¼ cups sugar

1¼ teaspoon ground cinnamon

½ teaspoon kosher salt

¼ cup dark raisins

½ cup golden raisins

6 ounces (about ¾ cup) cream cheese

6 ounces (about ¾ cup) mascarpone cheese

Flour, for dusting

1 pound all-butter frozen puff pastry, defrosted according to manufacturer's directions

1 egg beaten with 1 tablespoon water and a pinch of salt, for egg wash

Confectioners' sugar, for garnish

Vanilla ice cream

OAXACAN CHOCOLATE FONDUE
WITH CHURROS AND PASSION FRUIT MARSHMALLOWS

This tempting recipe is easily doubled to feed a great crowd of friends who, we assure you, won't be able to stop celebrating two Mexican treasures: Oaxaca's cinnamon-scented chocolate (see sidebar, page 190) in the fondue and crunchy, fried *Churros*. For added pleasure, we serve this fondue with delectable Passion Fruit Marshmallows (which can be made a couple of days ahead of time) plus sliced strawberries and bananas.

PASSION FRUIT MARSHMALLOWS

½ cup passion fruit purée (see Sources)

4 teaspoons powdered gelatin

2 large egg whites

1⅓ cups sugar

¼ cup light corn syrup

¼ cup water

Confectioners' sugar

FONDUE

2 cups heavy cream

½ cup egg yolks

4 (3-ounce) disks Mexican chocolate, finely ground in a food processor

1½ cups best-quality bittersweet chocolate, such as Valrhona

Churros (page 151)

3 cups sliced bananas and strawberries, for garnish

Serves 8

MAKE THE PASSION FRUIT MARSHMALLOWS: In a small bowl, mash the passion fruit purée until smooth. Sprinkle on the gelatin and let it soften. Put the egg whites in the bowl of a stand mixer fitted with the whisk attachment.

In a saucepan, combine the sugar, corn syrup, and water and bring to a full boil. Pour the sugar mixture into the bowl with the gelatin and fruit purée and whisk vigorously until the mixture triples in volume. Continue mixing until cooled.

Beat the egg whites on high speed until they form stiff peaks. Fold the purée and gelatin into the egg whites and whip on high speed for 5 minutes until the bowl has cooled to room temperature.

Line a baking sheet with parchment paper and cover with a thin layer of confectioners' sugar. Fill a pastry bag fitted with a medium-size plain tip with the egg white mixture. Pipe the mixture in 1 to 1½-inch circles on the baking sheet, raising your hands in the center so that a small peak forms. Let the marshmallows set for 2 hours, or until dry, before storing them on layers of parchment paper in an airtight container. Dust with confectioners' sugar before serving.

MAKE THE FONDUE: Pour the cream into the top of a double boiler, set it over simmering water, and heat until warm. Add the yolks, whisking continuously, until they have thickened enough to coat the back of a wooden spoon. Immediately remove the top of the pan and add both chocolates, whisking until they are well incorporated. Pour the chocolate mixture through a large strainer into a clean metal bowl, set aside, and keep warm over barely simmering water.

Make the *churros*.

Pour the warm chocolate fondue into a bowl. Serve with plates of marshmallows and a bowl of diced fruit with *churros* on the side.

KIWI-MARGARITA RASPADO
WITH FRUIT CEVICHE

Raspado means "shaved" or "scraped" in Spanish. In this version, the flavored liquid is frozen and scraped several times to form crunchy crystals of frozen liquid, like a granita, that are quite refreshing. This margarita-flavored *raspado* is a refreshing complement to the uncooked fruit salad. For the fruit ceviche (a play on how fish or vegetable ceviches are sliced and marinated), choose fruits that appeal to you and that are at the height of ripeness.

Serves 8 or more

MAKE THE RASPADO: In a small saucepan, combine the water and sugar, bring to a simmer, and then remove from the heat and refrigerate until cool.

Combine the sugar mixture with all of the *raspado* ingredients in a large bowl. Pour the mixture into a metal pan and freeze until just frozen but not rock hard. Remove the pan from the freezer and scrape the ice with a fork several times to stir up the ice crystals. Return the pan to the freezer and repeat this process 4 or 5 times, until you have a nice granular ice mixture.

MAKE THE FRUIT CEVICHE: In a small bowl, stir the sugar and lime juice together to dissolve the sugar. Stir in the Triple Sec and tequila. Combine the fruits in a large bowl, pour the lime juice mixture over the fruit, and toss gently. Before serving, sprinkle on the toasted coconut and toss again. Serve in dessert bowls with some *raspado* on top.

KIWI-MARGARITA RASPADO

¾ cup water

¾ cup sugar

¾ pound fresh kiwis, peeled and puréed

½ cup freshly squeezed lime juice

¼ cup good-quality silver tequila (see sidebar, page 197)

FRUIT CEVICHE

¼ cup sugar

2 tablespoons freshly squeezed lime juice

3 tablespoons Triple Sec or Curaçao

2 tablespoons good-quality silver tequila, (see sidebar, page 197)

4 cups finely diced ripe honeydew melon

3 large bananas, peeled and finely diced

1 large (about 1¼-pound) mango, peeled and finely diced (see sidebar, page 149)

1 cup dark sweet cherries, split and pitted

1 cup shredded sweetened coconut, lightly toasted (see page 152)

RASPADOS

In Mexico, there are carts all over the streets selling assorted flavors of *raspados* in the summertime. Generally, they are surrounded by droves of children. The cones are similar to snow cones made with compacted shaved ice and drizzled with sweetened syrup.

CHOCOLATE LAYER CAKE
WITH MORITA CHILE MOUSSE AND PISTACHIO PALANQUETTA

This spicy, sweet, rich, and creamy chocolate layer cake has a uniquely seductive hint of smoky morita chiles in the mousse filling along with crunchy bits of pistachio *palanquetta*, or brittle. While chocolate and chiles are used repeatedly in *mole* sauces, the combination adds a contemporary Mexican spin to this decadently delicious dessert. Although it takes time to prepare, like the greatest seductions, you will be rewarded. Omit the chiles if you don't feel adventurous. The brittle can be made ahead and stored in an airtight container for several days. You will need a half-sheet pan (about 17 by 11 by 1 inches) to bake the cake and a loaf pan (about 9 by 5 by 3 inches deep) in which to assemble it.

MORITA CHILE MOUSSE

4 cups heavy cream
2 to 4 morita chiles, stemmed and seeded (see Glossary)
1 cup finely chopped best-quality bittersweet European chocolate, such as Valrhona
3 (3-ounce) disks Mexican chocolate, finely ground in a food processor
2 large eggs, plus 4 egg yolks and 2 egg whites

CHOCOLATE CAKE

16 tablespoons (2 sticks) unsalted butter
2¼ cups sugar, plus 1¼ cups for the pistachio brittle
½ cup cocoa powder
4 large eggs
1¾ cups all-purpose flour
½ teaspoon kosher salt
½ teaspoon baking powder
½ teaspoon baking soda
2 cups warm water

1 cups shelled pistachios

½ cup Simple Syrup (page 187)
½ cup freshly squeezed orange juice
Pistachio or vanilla ice cream

Serves 8

MAKE THE MOUSSE: In a small saucepan over medium-high heat, combine the cream and morita chiles. Bring to a simmer, and then remove the pan from the heat, cover with plastic wrap, and let the chiles infuse for 20 minutes. Remove the chiles and discard. Refrigerate the cream.

In the top of a double boiler, melt the bittersweet chocolate over simmering water, stirring constantly until melted. Add the Mexican chocolate and stir until smooth. Let cool briefly.

In a large bowl, whisk the 2 whole eggs and 4 egg yolks until smooth. While beating constantly, pour the eggs into the melted chocolate and whisk until smooth.

In the bowl of a stand mixer fitted with the whisk attachment or with a whisk, beat the egg whites into soft peaks. Using a rubber spatula, scrape them into the egg-chocolate mixture, folding just until blended.

Beat the chile-infused cream into soft peaks and fold it into the mousse mixture with a rubber spatula. Cover and refrigerate the mousse.

MAKE THE CAKE: Preheat the oven to 325°F. Spray a half-sheet pan with nonstick vegetable spray and line the bottom with parchment paper.

In a large bowl and using a handheld electric mixer, cream the butter and 2¼ cups of the sugar until smooth. Stir in the cocoa powder. Beat in the eggs one at a time.

turning to coat evenly, and then scrape them onto the baking sheet, and let them cool until the caramel is hard. Turn the nut brittle onto a cutting board, coarsely chop with a sharp knife, and set aside.

Spray a loaf pan with nonstick spray. Line the pan with a piece of parchment paper long enough to extend 2 inches beyond the top edges on both long sides of the pan, and smooth it against the pan.

Cover the cooled cake with a piece of parchment paper and invert it onto a cutting board. Peel off the parchment from the cake. Trim the edges from the cake, and cut it into four equal rectangles, each measuring about 4 by 9 inches, to fit in the loaf pan. Combine the Simple Syrup and orange juice in a small bowl and dab the mixture liberally on the rectangles of cake.

Lay one rectangle in the pan. Using an offset spatula, spread one fourth of the mousse evenly over the top. Sprinkle on one-quarter of the pistachio brittle. Repeat with the remaining three layers of cake and pistachio brittle. Cover the pan with plastic wrap or aluminum foil and put in the freezer until firm enough to slice, at least 1 hour. (You can leave it in the freezer for up to 3 days.)

Remove the cake from the freezer, uncover, and let thaw for about 30 minutes. Using a sharp, thin-bladed knife, trace around the edges of the pan and carefully lift out the cake. Remove the parchment paper. From one narrow end, slice off a small triangular wedge (about ½ inch wide) at a slight angle. Slice the remaining cake into triangles, about 2¼ inches wide, using alternating cuts. You will have another ½-inch wedge at the other end. Serve with a scoop of pistachio or vanilla ice cream.

Combine the flour, salt, baking powder, and baking soda in another bowl, add them to the batter, and beat until just blended. Slowly add the water, beating continuously, until it is completely absorbed.

Scrape the batter into the prepared pan and bake for 10 minutes, turn the pan back to front, and bake for 5 minutes more, or until the surface of the cake is firm when lightly pressed in the center with your finger and the edges begin to pull away from the pan. Transfer the cake to a rack to cool.

MAKE THE BRITTLE: Line a baking sheet with parchment paper and spray with nonstick spray or spread with a little butter.

In a heavy-bottomed saucepan, heat ½ cup of the remaining 1¼ cups of sugar for the pistachio brittle over medium-high heat until golden, stirring constantly so that the sugar melts evenly. Continue adding the sugar, a little at a time, until the melted liquid is light brown. Stir in the pistachios,

CHOCOLATE BANANA PASTEL DE TRES LECHES

The *tres leches* in this beloved Oaxacan *pastel* are homogenized, evaporated, and condensed milks that together give the cake its name. Once the sponge cake is soaked in this liquid, it has a velvety texture and rich taste. Our dressed-up version is flavored with chocolate and has a lustrous caramelized banana topping.

8 tablespoons (1 stick) unsalted butter

½ cup firmly packed light brown sugar

2 tablespoons Grand Marnier or other orange-flavored liqueur

6 firm, ripe bananas

3 large eggs

¾ cup plus ¼ cup granulated sugar

4 cups plus ½ cup whole milk

½ cup plain whole-milk yogurt

2 tablespoons canola oil

½ teaspoon vanilla extract

1 cup cake flour

½ cup plus 1 tablespoon cocoa powder

1 teaspoon baking powder

¾ cup egg whites

1 (12-ounce) can evaporated milk

1 (12-ounce) can sweetened condensed milk

2 (3-ounce) disks Mexican chocolate, finely chopped or ground in a food processor

Serves 8

Preheat the oven to 325°F. Butter a nonstick 8-inch round cake pan.

In a large skillet, melt the butter over medium heat. Stir in the brown sugar and cook until the mixture becomes syrupy. Add the Grand Marnier and stir until blended. Immediately pour the caramel into the cake pan, turning the pan to spread the caramel evenly. Once the caramel has set, slice the bananas and lay them in an overlapping pattern to completely cover the bottom of the pan.

In a large bowl, beat the eggs, ¾ cup of the sugar, ½ cup of the milk, the yogurt, the oil, and the vanilla together until smooth. On a piece of waxed paper, sift together the flour, ½ cup of the cocoa, and the baking powder and gently fold it into the batter until just blended.

In a separate bowl, with a handheld electric mixer or whisk, beat the egg whites and the remaining ¼ cup of sugar into soft peaks and then gently fold them into the batter. Scrape the batter into the prepared pan with the bananas, spreading it evenly with a metal spatula.

Put the cake pan on a baking sheet, and bake in the middle of the oven. After 15 minutes, rotate the cake a half turn, and cook for 5 minutes more, or until golden brown and a toothpick comes out clean when it is inserted near the center. Remove the pan and cool on a rack.

Meanwhile, in a saucepan over medium-high heat, combine the remaining 4 cups of the whole milk and the evaporated milk and bring just to a boil. Remove from the heat, add the condensed milk and chocolate, and stir until smooth. Pour the liquid into a dish at least 10 inches wide by 2 inches deep and let cool.

Once the cake is cool, use a serrated knife to slice the top of the cake even with the top of the pan. Pierce the cake surface several times with a fork. Warm the bottom of the pan on top of the stove long enough to melt the caramel and release the bananas. Invert the cake into the dish with the milk, remove the pan, and let the caramel drip over the cake. Leave the cake to soak for 10 to 15 minutes to absorb the liquid. Using a serrated knife, cut the cake into wedges, and serve with a spatula.

FRIED KAHLÚA ICE CREAM BALLS
WITH RASPBERRY SAUCE

These crunchy-coated Kahlúa-flavored ice cream balls with chocolate are a real fiesta! The fast-fried ice cream is served in a bowl with barely cooked raspberries and cream. Dessert doesn't get any better than this! For a quick version, or if you don't have an ice cream maker, make the balls with premium quality, purchased coffee–chocolate chip ice cream. And, yes, you could also top the ice cream balls with hot chocolate sauce.

6 large egg yolks

1½ cups sugar

½ teaspoon kosher salt

2½ cups heavy cream

1½ cups milk

1 cup Kahlúa or other coffee liqueur

½ cup brewed espresso coffee, cooled

1 vanilla bean, split, with the seeds scraped

12 ounces bittersweet chocolate, chopped

1 cup all-purpose flour

3 large eggs, beaten

6 cups sweetened corn flakes and/or crisped rice cereal, finely chopped in a food processor

continued on next page

Serves 8

In the bowl of a stand mixer fitted with a whisk attachment, or with a handheld electric mixer, combine the egg yolks, sugar, and salt, and beat on high until doubled in volume.

In a large saucepan over medium heat, combine the heavy cream, milk, Kahlúa, espresso, and the vanilla bean pod and its seeds, bring to a simmer, and then remove from the heat and set aside.

With the mixer on low speed, very slowly pour the hot liquid into the egg yolk mixture, beating constantly until well blended. Return the mixture to the pan. Heat and stir continuously over low heat until the mixture is slightly thickened and coats the back of a wooden spoon. Strain it into a bowl and cool over an ice bath or in the refrigerator.

Once the liquid is cool, pour it into an ice cream maker and freeze according to the manufacturer's directions until semifrozen but not completely firm.

Meanwhile, melt the chocolate in the top of a double boiler or in a metal bowl set over gently boiling water, stirring until smooth. Remove from the heat and let the chocolate cool to room temperature.

Remove the top from the ice cream maker, and using a slotted spoon, drizzle the chocolate over the ice cream, stirring to create chocolate ribbons. Put the top back on the machine and finish freezing completely. Transfer the ice cream to the freezer and chill overnight until very firm.

Using three small bowls, put the flour in one, the eggs in another, and the cereal in the third. Using a large ice cream scoop, scoop a ball of ice cream. Quickly roll the ball in the flour, then in the eggs, and then in the cereal. Return the balls to the freezer on a flat dish or baking sheet to refreeze, and then dip the balls into the egg and cereal once more for a second coating.

MAKE THE RASPBERRY SAUCE: In a small saucepan, combine the sugar and water and bring to a boil. Remove from the heat, gently stir in the raspberries, and steep until cool while frying the ice cream.

Beat the heavy cream into soft peaks and sweeten with sugar. Divide the raspberries among 8 dessert bowls.

In a small, deep saucepan, heat enough oil to cover the ice cream balls to 325°F and quickly fry each ice cream ball just until the outside is crispy, less than 1 minute.
Put the ice cream balls in the bowls with the raspberries, add a generous dollop of whipped cream to each, and serve immediately.

RASPBERRY SAUCE

1 cup sugar

1 cup water

1 pint raspberries

1 cup heavy cream, whipped into peaks and
    sweetened with sugar, for garnish

1 to 2 cups canola oil, for frying

DESAYUNO

Chapter Seven: **BREAKFAST AND BRUNCH**

EL DESAYUNO (BREAKFAST) in Mexico is

one of the most important meals of the day. Because it is so hearty, at Dos Caminos we serve it for our weekend brunch. Typically it begins with *pan dulces*, like *Conchas,* the traditional Mexican sweet breads that are dunked in hot beverages like *Champurrado* or *Café de Olla*.

Dishes like as *Huevos Rancheros*—here, fried eggs served over a crisp tortilla with serrano ham and roasted tomato salsa—and the cheesy tortilla casserole known as *Chilaquiles* are some of my favorite savory dishes. But if you prefer something sweeter, I've also included my unique take on pancakes and French toast coated with crispy rice cereal. *¡Buenos días!*

BANANA PANCAKES
WITH PILONCILLO SYRUP AND SPICED CREMA

Piloncillo (see Glossary), or Mexican raw sugar, is used to make the delicious spiced syrup that is ladled over these generously sized pancakes, which make a festive Sunday brunch. While pancakes themselves are not a traditional dish in Mexico, I see the flavors and seasonings in this recipe as being true to somewhere like Veracruz, which is a tropical region famous for its spices and vanilla beans. Toast the pecans in the oven or in a toaster oven at 350°F for 5 to 6 minutes, shaking the pan a couple of times.

Serves 4 to 6 (12 pancakes)

MAKE THE BATTER: In a large bowl, whisk the eggs, milk, oil, and vanilla together until smooth. Combine the dry ingredients in another large bowl and then whisk them into the liquid mixture until just incorporated. Gently fold the bananas into the batter, cover, and refrigerate for 1 hour to rest.

MAKE THE SYRUP: In a medium-size saucepan over medium heat, combine the water, *piloncillo*, star anise, and cinnamon. Bring to a simmer and cook until the liquid reaches a syrupy consistency, about 10 minutes. Remove the spices, stir in the toasted pecans, and keep warm.

MAKE THE SPICED CREMA: In a medium-size bowl, whisk the ingredients for the crema into soft peaks.

Preheat a griddle or skillet over medium-high heat and brush with butter. Pour ⅓ cup of the batter for each pancake onto the griddle or into the skillet, cook until little bubbles form on the surface, about 3 minutes, turn with a spatula, and cook the second side for about the same time, until lightly browned. Serve the pancakes topped with a dollop of Spiced Crema and the warm *piloncillo* syrup on the side.

BATTER

4 large eggs, beaten
½ cup milk
¼ cup canola oil
½ teaspoon vanilla extract
¼ teaspoon ground ginger
3 cups all-purpose flour
¾ cup light brown sugar
1 teaspoon baking powder
½ teaspoon kosher salt
½ pound very ripe bananas, peeled and mashed

SYRUP

1 cup water
½ pound finely chopped piloncillo or firmly packed dark brown sugar
1 star anise
1 stick cinnamon, preferably Mexican
½ cup toasted, chopped pecans

SPICED CREMA

1 cup heavy cream
2 tablespoons mascarpone or cream cheese
¼ cup confectioners' sugar
⅛ teaspoon ground allspice
⅛ teaspoon ground cinnamon

1 tablespoon unsalted butter, melted, for cooking the pancakes

CONCHAS
PAN DULCE

In Mexico, *pan dulce* is served in the morning with coffee or hot chocolate. There are many types of these little pastries, and the smell outside the *panadería,* or bread shop, in the morning is among my fondest memories from my travels in Mexico. *Concha* is the Spanish word for "seashell." These small, round sweet breads are topped with crispy sugar striped with a design that makes them resemble shells. The same dough is used for *Pan de Muerto.*

2 packages active dry yeast

½ cup warm water

4 large eggs, plus 2 egg yolks and 4 egg whites

½ cup milk

6 cups all-purpose flour

¾ cup sugar, plus 1 cup for glaze

2 tablespoons finely grated orange zest

2 teaspoons ground anise

1 teaspoon kosher salt a

8 tablespoons (1 stick) unsalted butter, softened

Makes 8 rolls

In a small bowl, sprinkle the yeast over the warm water, and let stand until small bubbles form at the edge, about 10 minutes. In another small bowl, whisk together the 4 whole eggs, 2 egg yolks, and milk.

In a large bowl, mix 5 cups of the flour with ¾ cup of the sugar, the orange zest, anise, and salt. Using a pastry cutter or two knives, cut in the butter until the mixture looks crumbly. Pour in the dissolved yeast and mix until blended. Add the milk-egg mixture and knead for about 10 minutes, or until the dough is smooth and elastic, adding some of the remaining 1 cup of flour, as needed. Roll the dough into a ball, put it into a greased bowl, turn once, cover with a damp towel, and let it rise in a warm place for 1½ hours.

After the dough has risen the first time, punch it down, cut it into 3- to 4-ounce pieces, and roll into balls. Each ball should be about 2½ to 3 inches in diameter.

PAN DE MUERTO
BREAD FOR EL DÍA DE LOS MUERTOS

The traditional sweet bread served on *El Día de los Muertos* uses the same dough recipe as *Conchas* to make 2 (1-pound) loaves. After the first rising, the dough is punched down and typically formed into loaves shaped like logs or skulls (with strips of dough attached to look like bones) and left to rise for another hour. Rather than using 1 cup of sugar and 4 egg whites to glaze the breads (as in *Conchas*), a glaze is made by heating ½ cup orange juice and ½ cup finely chopped *piloncillo* or firmly packed dark brown sugar in a small saucepan over medium heat until the sugar melts. It is brushed on after 40 minutes of baking. The loaves are then baked for 5 to 10 minutes more until golden brown and baked through. Let the loaves rest briefly and then serve warm.

In a small bowl, whisk the egg whites and remaining 1 cup of sugar until they begin to get airy and fluffy.

Lightly grease a baking sheet and place the balls about 2 inches apart. With the palm of your hand, gently flatten each ball. With a pastry brush, brush a generous amount of the egg-sugar mixture over the top of each roll. Then, with the tines of a fork, make crisscross marks across the top of each. Bake for 20 to 25 minutes, or until golden brown and cooked through. Remove, let stand briefly, then serve warm.

EL DÍA DE LOS MUERTOS

El Día de los Muertos, or the Day of the Dead, is an ancient celebration that dates back thousands of years to Aztec, Mayan, and other early indigenous civilizations. In pre-Hispanic times, skulls were commonly displayed as trophies during rituals symbolizing death and rebirth. After the Spanish conquest of Mexico, Catholic priests moved the celebrations to coincide with All Saints' Day (November 1) and All Souls' Day (November 2) on the Christian calendar.

Although death is considered macabre in some cultures, Mexicans believe that it is time for a lively party and to remember that death is the beginning of yet another stage in life for their relatives. Plans for the celebration are made throughout the year. From October 31 to November 2, families gather at the graves of relatives to clean them and decorate them with offerings like bottles of tequila or mezcal, colorfully decorated sugar skulls and candies, and *Pan de Muerto*. Frequently they include vibrant orange marigolds, the *flor* (flower) *de muerto*. All are thought to attract the spirit of the dead. For children, the offerings frequently include toys.

Some well-to-do families also build altars or shrines in their homes that are decorated with pictures of departed relatives, candles, and a crucifix. The colorful traditions vary dramatically throughout Mexico but they are all characterized by a blend of traditional, pre-Hispanic Mexican and

HUEVOS RANCHEROS
RANCHERS' EGGS

The perfect south-of-the-border dish to wake up your taste buds! Serve these ranchers' eggs for brunch or even late for a midnight supper. Sunny-side up eggs are traditional, but do them any style you want.

RANCHERO SAUCE

½ pound sliced bacon

6 medium plum tomatoes

2 red bell peppers

2 poblano chiles

2 tablespoons canola oil

1 medium yellow onion, diced

6 cloves garlic, chopped

¼ cup tomato paste

2 canned chipotle chiles in adobo

4 cups chicken stock

Kosher salt

1 cup canola oil, for frying

6 (6-inch) corn tortillas, purchased or homemade (page 9)

2 cups Frijoles Refritos (page 135) or canned refried beans, warmed

12 thin slices serrano or any other type of ham

6 ounces Chihuahua cheese or Monterey Jack cheese, grated (about 1½ cups)

12 large eggs

8 ounces queso fresco, crumbled (about 2 cups)

2 firm, ripe avocados, peeled and diced

Pico de gallo (page 2)

Serves 6

Preheat the oven to 350°F.

Lay the pieces of bacon flat in a jelly-roll pan or half-sheet pan, and bake until crisp, about 15 minutes. Remove the bacon, drain on paper towels, and chop into small pieces. Leave the oven on.

On a baking sheet, roast the tomatoes until the skins blister, about 10 minutes. Remove the tomatoes, coarsely chop, and set aside.

Roast the bell peppers and poblano chiles over high heat, directly on a gas burner, over an open flame, or under the broiler, until the skins begin to blister and turn black. Use tongs to turn them so that they are charred all over. Transfer them to a bowl, cover tightly with plastic wrap until cooled, and then carefully scrape off the skins. Cut a slit from the stem toward the tip and remove the seeds and membranes, and then dice.

Heat a medium saucepan over medium heat. Add the oil and the onion, and sauté until lightly browned, 3 to 4 minutes. Add the garlic, and continue to cook for 1 minute more. Stir in the tomato paste, cook for 1 to 2 minutes, and then add the roasted tomatoes, chipotles, and chicken stock, and simmer for 10 minutes. Transfer the mixture to the jar of an electric blender and purée until smooth. Add the chopped bacon and roasted diced peppers to the finished tomato sauce, season to taste with salt, and keep hot.

In a large skillet, heat the oil until hot. Add the tortillas one at a time, and fry until pliable, about 1 minute per side. Remove from the pan, drain on paper towels, and continue with the remaining tortillas. Wipe out the skillet with paper towels.

Spoon ¼ cup of the refried beans in the center of each of six plates. Put 1 tortilla on top of the beans and top with two slices of ham and ¼ cup of grated cheese.

In the skillet, immediately cook the eggs sunny-side up, just until the yolks are set. Put two eggs on each plate on top of the ham and pour about ½ cup of hot Ranchero Sauce over the top. Sprinkle with crumbled *queso fresco*, add a few pieces of avocado and some pico de gallo, and serve.

SINCRONIZADAS CON HUEVOS
MEXICAN HAM AND CHEESE QUESADILLAS

A cousin of quesadillas, *sincronizadas* are typically made with two tortillas held together by melted cheese and sliced ham, like a sandwich. They are a popular Mexican breakfast item and are very easy to make. I like to use thinly sliced serrano ham from Spain, but any kind of ham will work. Dress them up with a tempting Roasted Poblano Hollandaise.

ROASTED POBLANO HOLLANDAISE

16 tablespoons (2 sticks) unsalted butter

2 large egg yolks

1½ tablespoons warm water

1 tablespoon freshly squeezed lemon juice

Kosher salt

½ cup roasted, peeled, seeded, and diced
    poblano chiles

¼ cup chopped fresh cilantro leaves

SINCRONIZADAS

Frijoles Refritos (page 135)

3 (12-inch) purchased flour tortillas

12 ounces serrano or any other ham, thinly
    sliced

12 ounces Chihuahua, Cheddar, or Monterey
    Jack cheese, grated (about 3 cups)

4 tablespoons unsalted butter, softened

continued on next page

Serves 6

Prepare the *Frijoles Refritos*.

MAKE THE HOLLANDAISE: Melt the butter and keep it warm but not hot. In the top of a double boiler, beat the egg yolks, water, and lemon juice until blended. Set the bowl over about 1 inch of simmering water and whisk continuously until the yolks become light and fluffy, about 5 minutes.

Remove the top from the pan and continue whisking until the mixture cools slightly. Slowly drizzle the butter into the egg mixture, whisking constantly. If the mixture becomes too hot or too cold, it will break—it should remain around 120°F, or warm to the touch. Season to taste with salt. Add the chiles and, just before serving, add the cilantro. Keep the hollandaise sauce warm in a double boiler over warm water.

MAKE THE SINCRONIZADAS: Preheat the oven to 250°F. Preheat a griddle or large nonstick skillet until hot.

Spread one side of each flour tortilla with about 2 tablespoons of *Frijoles Refritos*. Divide the sliced ham and cheese equally among the tortillas, laying them on top of the beans. Fold the tortillas in half. Spread the softened butter over the outer surfaces of the tortillas, and cook on the griddle or in a large skillet, as you would a grilled cheese sandwich, until the cheese melts inside and the outsides are brown and crispy, turning once. Transfer the cooked *sincronizadas* to the oven to keep warm.

Meanwhile, poach the eggs. Fill a medium-size pan with at least 3 inches of water, bring to a boil, and then reduce the heat so that only small bubbles occasionally break the surface. Add about 1 teaspon of white vinegar or lemon juice to the water to help hold the whites together. Break each egg into a small cup or bowl. Carefully slide the eggs individually into the water. Don't put too many eggs in the pot at one time.

Immediately cover the pan and turn off the heat. Let the eggs stand for 3 to 4 minutes for medium yolks. Adjust the time up or down for firmer or runnier yolks. When the eggs are cooked, transfer them to a bowl of hot but not boiling water. If the water cools, add more hot water. Once all the eggs are cooked and you are ready to serve, remove them with a slotted spoon and drain on paper towels.

Cut the *sincronizadas* into four pieces. Serve 2 pieces per person. Top each piece with a poached egg and 2 tablespoons of Roasted Poblano Hollandaise. Garnish with pico de gallo and serve.

12 large eggs
2 to 3 teaspoons red wine vinegar
Pico de gallo (page 2), for garnish

CHORIZO CON HUEVOS

Scrambled eggs and sausages done Mexican style boast plenty of *brava*. Once the chorizo is browned, leave as much or little of the fat as you like (but at least 3 tablespoons) in the pan in which to cook the eggs. It imparts a great flavor.

Serves 6

Heat a medium-size nonstick skillet over medium-high heat. Add the chorizo and cook until the pieces are lightly browned and the fat is rendered, breaking up the pieces with a wooden spatula. Remove all but 3 tablespoons of fat, pour in the eggs, season to taste with salt and pepper, and cook to desired degree of doneness.

Discard about half the fat from the pan. Reheat the skillet over medium-high heat, add the eggs and chorizo, and cook until done to your taste. Divide among 6 individual plates. Serve with *Frijoles Refritos* sprinkled with a little grated *cotija* cheese, sliced avocados, warm tortillas, and pico de gallo.

1 pound Mexican chorizo, casings removed, chopped
Kosher salt and freshly ground black pepper
12 large eggs, beaten until smooth

2 cups Frijoles Refritos (page 135), or canned refried beans, warmed
2 ounces cotija or feta cheese, grated (about ½ cup)
1 ripe avocado, peeled and sliced
6 to 12 (6-inch) corn tortillas, purchased or homemade (page 9), warmed
Pico de gallo (page 2)

PAN TORREJAS

Mexican-style French toast with a creamy custard-like interior and crunchy outside is a treat. We add a dollop of whipped cream on top and serve it with maple berry syrup. To better absorb the eggs and cream, use day-old brioche or egg bread. If your loaf is fresh, cut the loaf into 1½-inch thick slices and let them stand uncovered for a few hours.

Serves 6

Cut the brioche into 6 (1½-inch-thick) slices. In a large bowl, combine the eggs, milk, 3 cups of the cream, 1 cup of the sugar, cinnamon, ginger, and vanilla and beat until smooth. Add the sliced brioche to the batter and let the slices soak until completely saturated with the liquid.

Meanwhile, put the cereal into a plastic freezer bag and crush into a coarse coating using your hands. Pour the cereal into a flat dish or pie plate. Dip each slice of soaked bread in the cereal, turning to coat it evenly.

Preheat the oven to 250°F.

In a large, nonstick skillet over medium heat, melt 1 to 2 tablespoons of the butter. Add as many slices of the soaked bread as will fit comfortably in the pan without crowding and cook until golden brown, 2 to 3 minutes per side, turning once. Transfer the cooked slices to a baking sheet and keep warm in the oven while cooking the remaining bread, adding more butter to the skillet as needed.

Once all of the toast is cooked, in a bowl, beat the remaining 1 cup of heavy cream and 1 tablespoon of sugar into soft peaks and set aside. In a saucepan, combine the maple syrup and berries, bring just to a simmer, remove from the heat, and let stand for a few minutes. Cut each slice of toast in half diagonally and divide among six individual plates. Garnish with whipped cream and warm berry syrup.

1 (about 1-pound) day-old rectangular loaf of brioche or egg bread

8 large eggs

3 cups milk

3 cups heavy cream, plus 1 cup for whipped cream

1 cup sugar, plus 1 tablespoon for whipped cream

1 teaspoon ground cinnamon

½ teaspoon ground ginger

1 teaspoon vanilla extract

4 cups crisp rice cereal

4 tablespoons unsalted butter

2 cups maple syrup

2 cups mixed berries (such as raspberries, sliced strawberries, and blueberries)

CHILAQUILES

This crunchy-chewy baked tortilla casserole is commonly made with leftover tortilla chips, various meat fillings, sour cream, and cheese. It is sort of a cross between nachos and enchiladas—slightly crispy and deliciously gooey. Sometimes the casserole is topped with fried eggs, as well. It is eaten at any time of the day, but it is especially welcome for breakfast or brunch. In Mexico, it is also said to be a common remedy for a hangover. You can use either two 2-quart casseroles or one 4-quart dish to bake and serve this. Also, it can be baked up to 2 hours ahead and reheated.

RES CHILES SALSA

5 ancho chiles, peeled

5 guajillo chiles

3 arbol chiles

2 cups cooking liquid, reserved from soaking the chiles

6 cloves garlic

4 plum tomatoes

1 medium-size yellow onion, quartered

1 tablespoon olive oil

Kosher salt and freshly ground black pepper

CHILAQUILES

1 large bag tortilla chips

1½ cups sour cream

8 ounces Chihuahua cheese or Monterey Jack cheese, grated (about 2 cups)

12 large eggs

1 cup finely chopped fresh cilantro leaves

4 ounces cotija or feta cheese, finely grated, for garnish (about 1 cup)

2 avocados peeled, seeded, and cut into ½-inch cubes

6 Jalapeños en Escabeche (page 144) or purchased pickled jalapeño chiles in a jar or can

Serves 6

MAKE THE TRES CHILES SALSA: Preheat the oven to 400°F.

Toast and rehydrate the chiles (see page 6), using at least 3 cups of water. Let the chiles cool in the cooking liquid. Remove the chiles, and reserve 2 cups of the cooking liquid.

Toss the garlic, tomatoes, and onion with the olive oil, and bake on a baking sheet for 10 minutes, or until the onions are soft. Place all of the ingredients in the jar of an electric blender, adding only as little of the liquid as needed to purée until smooth. Season to taste with salt and black pepper, and set aside. Leave the oven on.

MAKE THE CHILAQUILES: In 2 (2-quart) casseroles, add half of the tortilla chips, half of the salsa, and half of the sour cream to each, and stir together with half of the Chihuahua cheese. Bake the casseroles in the oven for 3 minutes, and then remove and top with the remaining cheese and sauce. Return to the oven and bake for 3 minutes more.

While the casseroles bake, scramble the eggs or fry them sunny-side up, and keep them warm.

Remove the casseroles from the oven. Place a heaping spoonful of *chilaquiles* on each plate, top with 2 eggs, and spoon some of the remaining salsa around the eggs. Sprinkle with the cilantro and *cotija* cheese and serve the avocado cubes and jalapeño chiles on the side.

POTATO AND JICAMA PANCAKES
WITH SMOKED TROUT AND CREMA

These unique, tasty pancakes are small—the size of a silver peso or silver dollar. With matchstick pieces of jicama added to the grated potatoes, they look like little crunchy birds' nests. In the mountains of Oaxaca, I visited a famous trout farm, where we had this delicious delicacy in several different preparations at every meal.

Serves 8

MAKE THE BATTER: Preheat the oven to 375°F. Bake the potatoes until soft, about 1 hour. Remove and, when cool enough to handle, peel and coarsely grate.

Combine the potatoes with all the remaining ingredients, except the jicama and lemon juice, mix until smooth, and refrigerate for at least 1 hour. Meanwhile, peel the jicama, cut it into matchsticks, and put in a bowl of cold water with the lemon juice added. Just prior to making the pancakes, blot the jicama very dry on paper towels and gently fold it in to the batter.

Heat a griddle or large, nonstick skillet over medium-high heat. Brush with butter, pour in ¼ cup of batter, and cook for 2 to 3 minutes per side until golden brown, turning once. Serve 2 warm pancakes in the center of each of 8 plates. Add a tablespoon of smoked trout on top of each pancake, drizzle with a little crema, garnish with chopped scallions and arugula or watercress, and serve.

PANCAKE BATTER

2 russet or other baking potatoes

1¼ cups all-purpose flour

1 cup milk

6 large eggs

2 tablespoons canola oil

¼ cup chopped scallions, plus ¼ cup for garnish

¼ cup seeded and diced jalapeño chiles

1 teaspoon kosher salt

1½ teaspoons baking powder

½ pound jicama

Dash of freshly squeezed lemon juice

2 tablespoons unsalted butter, melted, for cooking the pancakes

1 pound smoked trout, skinned, bones removed, and flaked

½ cup crema (page 10) or sour cream

2 to 3 sliced scallions, including green parts, for garnish

Arugula or watercress sprigs, for garnish

CORN AND CHIPOTLE PANCAKES
WITH GRILLED LOBSTER AND ROASTED CORN PICO DE GALLO

If you love the taste of cornbread, you'll love these pancakes. Top them with lobster meat and Roasted Corn Pico de Gallo, and let the celebration begin.

PANCAKE BATTER

2 cups yellow cornmeal

2 cups all-purpose flour

1½ teaspoons baking powder

1 teaspoons kosher salt

½ cup buttermilk

½ cup milk

5 large eggs

6 tablespoons unsalted butter, melted, plus
    2 tablespoons to brush on lobsters and
    griddle

4 tablespoons honey

2 tablespoons canola oil

3 cups fresh corn kernels or defrosted high-
    quality frozen corn

2 canned chipotle chiles in adobo, chopped

½ cup chopped fresh cilantro leaves

ROASTED CORN PICO DE GALLO

2 cups roasted corn kernels (prepared
    earlier)

1 cup diced tomatoes

½ cup diced red onions

½ cup chopped fresh cilantro leaves

¼ cup diced jalapeño chiles

2 tablespoons freshly squeezed lime juice

¼ cup olive oil

Kosher salt

continued on next page

Serves 6

MAKE THE BATTER: In a large bowl, combine the cornmeal, flour, baking powder, and salt. In a separate bowl, combine the buttermilk, milk, eggs, 6 tablespoons of the butter, and honey, and whisk together until smooth.

Heat a large skillet over medium-high heat. Add the oil and the corn and sauté until the kernels are lightly browned and tender, about 5 minutes. Reserve 2 cups of the corn for the Roasted Corn Pico de Gallo.

Stir the remaining 1 cup of the corn, the chipotles, and the cilantro into the buttermilk mixture, add to the dry ingredients, and mix just until blended. Cover the batter and refrigerate for at least 1 hour before using.

While the batter rests, combine the remaining 2 cups of roasted corn with the other Roasted Corn Pico de Gallo ingredients in a bowl, season to taste with salt, cover, and refrigerate for at least 30 minutes.

Combine the crema, chipotles, and lime juice, and season to taste with salt.

In a large pot, bring at least 4 quarts of salted water to a rolling boil. Add the lobsters, cover the pot, return the water to a boil, and cook the lobsters for 7 minutes more, or until the shells are bright red. Remove the lobsters with tongs, wrap each in aluminum foil, and let cool. Break off the tails, cut them in half lengthwise, and remove the meat. Remove the claw meat whole and any remaining meat from the shells. Discard the shells or reserve for Lobster Stock (page 96). Brush the meat lightly with melted butter, season with salt and pepper, and sauté briefly in a large skillet to warm.

Heat a griddle or large nonstick skillet over medium-high heat. Brush with a little butter and ladle on enough batter to make 3- to 4-inch rounds. Cook the pancakes until little bubbles form on the surface and the bottom is golden brown, 1½ to 2 minutes. Turn with a spatula and cook the second side until golden brown.

On each of 6 plates, serve 2 pancakes, one garnished with half a lobster tail and the other with a claw. Spoon on some Roasted Corn Pico de Gallo, drizzle with crema, garnish with watercress sprigs, and serve.

1½ cups crema (page 10) or sour cream

2 canned chipotle chiles in adobo, puréed

1 tablespoon freshly squeezed lime juice

3 (1-pound) lobsters

Watercress sprigs, for garnish

SMOKED SALMON EGGS BENEDICT MEXICANO

This dish is usually prepared with ham, but silky smoked salmon is a nice alternative, served on cheesy cornbread with Chipotle Hollandaise Sauce. For the hollandaise, use the Roasted Poblano Hollandaise recipe on page 176, but omit the poblano chiles and cilantro, and replace them with 2 tablespoons of chopped canned chipotle chiles in adobo (see Glossary).

CORNBREAD

2 cups yellow cornmeal

2 cups all-purpose flour

2 tablespoons baking powder

2 teaspoons baking soda

2 teaspoons kosher salt

8 ounces Cheddar cheese, grated
(about 2 cups)

2 cups buttermilk

½ cup honey

6 large eggs

8 tablespoons (1 stick) unsalted butter, melted

4 tablespoons canned chipotle chiles in adobo, chopped

Chipotle Hollandaise Sauce (see headnote)

12 large eggs

1 pound asparagus, woody ends snapped off

1 pound thinly sliced smoked salmon

2 ripe avocados, peeled and thinly sliced

¼ cup chopped fresh cilantro leaves, for garnish

Serves 6

MAKE THE CORNBREAD: Preheat the oven to 375°F. Butter a nonstick 9 by 13-inch baking dish.

In a large bowl, combine the cornmeal, flour, baking powder, baking soda, and salt. Stir in the cheese. Whisk in the buttermilk, honey, eggs, melted butter, and chipotles, and blend just until smooth. Do not overmix. Scrape the batter into the prepared dish. Bake for 35 minutes, or until a toothpick inserted into the center comes out clean. Cool for 5 minutes and then turn the cornbread out onto a rack and cool completely. With a sharp knife, cut it into 2 by 2-inch pieces. Slice off the rounded top of each square as necessary so the poached eggs sit flat on the cornbread squares.

Meanwhile, make the Chipotle Hollandaise Sauce, and poach the eggs (see page 176). When the eggs are done, transfer them with a slotted spoon to a pan of hot but not boiling water. Steam the asparagus in a basket set over boiling water until bright green and crisp-tender, 5 to 6 minutes.

In the center of each of 6 large plates, serve 2 squares of cornbread, each topped with a couple of slices of avocado and 2 asparagus spears cut in half crosswise. Divide the salmon among the pieces of cornbread, and put an egg on top of each, spoon 2 tablespoons of Chipotle Hollandaise Sauce on top, garnish with a little cilantro, and serve.

BEBIDAS

Chapter Eight: **DRINKS**

WALK THROUGH ANY MARKET in Mexico

in the morning and you'll smell the pungent aroma of *champurrado*, or Mexican hot chocolate, and *Café de Olla*, the local, freshly brewed coffee scented with *canela* (cinnamon sticks). Many stalls also have large glass jugs filled with *aguas frescas* and *liquados,* fruit drinks made from local produce.

Throughout the day, you can quench your thirst with delicious hot, cold, or even frozen drinks. Among the most celebrated of these beverages are margaritas, the tequila-based cocktails. Genuine tequila is a distilled spirit made from the blue agave plant that grows in the region around the historic town of Tequila, in the state of Jalisco. Another distilled spirit, called *mezcal*, is made from similar varieties of this plant growing elsewhere in Mexico, but it cannot be called tequila.

Beyond margaritas and Bloody Marias (the classic spicy tomato juice cocktail made with tequila rather than vodka), tequila is increasingly becoming the spirit of choice with sophisticated drinkers across the United States. Like many Mexicans, Americans north of the border are drinking their tequila neat or with a squeeze of lime. This is where different types and styles of tequila are especially discernible. Some of the finest ones are aged up to three years in oak barrels and sipped like good cognac or whiskey.

There are many crisp, light, and refreshing drinks both alcoholic and nonalcoholic that pair well with Mexican food. Of course, an ice-cold beer with a squeeze of lime is a natural. In this chapter, I include some of my favorites drinks.

WATERMELON AGUA FRESCA

Serve this fresh fruit drink in pitchers, garnished with watermelon wedges and mint or lemon verbena sprigs floating on top. For extra credit, serve it as a punch in half of a scooped out watermelon. Not only is this *agua fresca* refreshing by itself, it is also great to keep around as a mixer for tequila, vodka, or white rum. It will keep for at least a week in the refrigerator.

Serves 8

MAKE THE SIMPLE SYRUP: In a small saucepan, combine the sugar and water. Bring to a gentle boil and stir until the sugar has completely dissolved. Remove from the heat and refrigerate until cool.

In the jar of an electric blender, purée the watermelon and orange juice until smooth. Pour through a fine mesh strainer, and stir in the lime juice and Simple Syrup. Pour into tall glasses, add ice cubes, and serve.

SIMPLE SYRUP

1 cup sugar

1 cup water

½ large watermelon, cut into chunks (about 16 cups)

2 cups freshly squeezed orange juice

1 cup freshly squeezed lime juice

ICED MINT TEA
WITH STRAWBERRIES

A refreshingly cool, light beverage to complement any Mexican meal. Rather than strawberries, you could use small cubes of peeled peaches.

Serves 8

In a large bowl, combine 2 cups of the mint leaves with the sugar, add the water, and steep for 5 minutes, stirring to dissolve the sugar, and let cool. Strain the liquid into a tall pitcher. Stir in the lime juice, strawberries, and the remaining ½ cup of mint leaves. Serve in tall glasses over ice.

2½ cups loosely packed fresh mint leaves

2 cups sugar

8 cups boiling water

2 tablespoons freshly squeezed lemon juice

2 cups sliced fresh strawberries

MANGO LIQUADO

Liquados are delightfully refreshing drinks made with very ripe fruit. I've had them everywhere from the beach in Playa del Carmen to the zócalo of Puebla. These smoothies, similar to their popular counterparts in the United States, have been popular in Mexico for decades. In cooler months, you can recapture a taste of tropical Mexico by using frozen ripe fruit. For an interesting twist, add vanilla frozen yogurt instead of the ice cubes.

Serves 4

In the jar of an electric blender, combine all of the ingredients except the mint and purée until smooth. Pour through a fine strainer into tall glasses, add mint, and serve.

4 cups diced fresh mango (see page 149) or unsweetened frozen pieces

2 cups freshly squeezed orange juice

2 cups ice

4 tablespoons freshly squeezed lime juice

4 small mint sprigs, for garnish

LIQUADO VARIATIONS

In addition to the fresh (or frozen) mango used here, you could use melons, bananas, pineapples, and any of several berries when they are at the peak of sweetness. To each cup of cut fruit, add 1 cup of ice water, a generous squeeze of fresh lime juice, and about 1 tablespoon of sugar, or to taste. Purée the mixture in an electric blender, strain into a tall glass, and serve.

MEXICAN HOT CHOCOLATE

Mexicans love hot chocolate for breakfast and at almost any time of the day. In this recipe we use half milk and half heavy cream for a richer texture, but you can use any variety of milk you prefer.

3 cups milk

3¾ cups heavy cream

1 cinnamon stick, preferably Mexican

Grated zest of 1 orange

½ cup finely chopped piloncillo or firmly packed dark brown sugar

3 (3-ounce) disks Mexican chocolate, grated or finely ground in a food processor

1 tablespoon sugar

Cocoa powder, for garnish

Serves 8

In a saucepan, combine the milk, 3 cups of the cream, the cinnamon, the orange zest, and the *piloncillo* and bring to a simmer, stirring to melt the sugar. Remove the pan from the heat.

Melt the chocolate in the top of a double boiler set over simmering water, and strain the milk-cream mixture into the chocolate, whisking until the chocolate is melted and smooth. Whip the remaining ¾ cup of cream with the sugar into soft peaks. Ladle the hot chocolate into cups or mugs. Garnish with a dollop of whipped cream and a dusting of cocoa powder.

OAXACA'S CHOCOLATE

The seductive smell of roasting cocoa beans and the sounds of those beans being ground into chocolate is part of everyday life in Oaxaca, in the Mexican state of the same name.

For centuries, cocoa beans—native to Chiapas and Tabasco in the south—have been brought here to be ground and prepared as a hot beverage. It is said that the average Oaxaqueño drinks at least five times more hot chocolate than the rest of the country. Try our Mexican Hot Chocolate or *Champurrado*, and you might be converted.

I experienced chocolate-making firsthand in Oaxaca at the Benito Juárez Market, southwest of the central square, or *zócalo*. It's been the site of Oaxaca's main market since the mid-seventeenth century, and chocolate grinders form a line of storefronts along the southern end of the market on 20 de Noviembre Street. Some of the most

well-known chocolate grinders include Mayordomo, La Soledad, and Guelaguetza. They sell everything chocolate, from the beans to chocolate bars and packaged instant hot chocolate drinks. I made the trip with some chef-friends to sample the local specialties, like *clayudas* (a big Mexican pizza) and chiles rellenos, drink big, steaming bowls of Oaxacan hot chocolate, and chat with the local vendors. As is typical in Mexico, each stand is run by an entire family.

Compared with dark, bittersweet European-style chocolates, Oaxacan chocolate is somewhat grainier because it is ground by hand or in old electric grinders along with sugar, cinnamon, roasted almonds, and sometimes vanilla. Proportions vary according to each manufacturer's recipe, and some families even have their own blends ground at local stores.

CHAMPURRADO
WITH MEZCAL WHIPPED CREAM

With a combination of European-style chocolate and cinnamon-scented Mexican chocolate and fine corn flour added, this version of hot chocolate is rich, with a thick texture. In Mexico, the drink is almost as thick as a cereal. *Champurrado* can be made several hours ahead and kept in the refrigerator, then heated as desired. We also serve it with crispy *Churros* (page 151).

Serves 6 to 8

In a medium-size stainless steel pot, combine the milk, cream, water, sugar, and vanilla, and bring to a simmer. Add both chocolates and stir until melted. Add the dissolved corn flour, and whisk until the mixture thickens slightly, about 10 minutes over low heat, stirring frequently.

While the chocolate is simmering, whip the cream. Using a handheld electric mixer or a stand mixer, beat the cream into soft peaks. Fold in the confectioners' sugar, mezcal, and vanilla. Serve the drink warm, garnished with whipped cream.

4 cups whole milk
1 cup heavy cream
1 cup water
½ cup sugar
1 vanilla bean, split and scraped, or 1
    teaspoon vanilla extract
2 (3-ounce) disks Mexican chocolate, grated
    or finely ground in a food processor
4 ounces bittersweet chocolate, chopped
2 tablespoons corn flour for tortillas,
    dissolved in ¼ cup warm water

MEZCAL WHIPPED CREAM

1 cup heavy cream
1½ tablespoons confectioners' sugar
2 tablespoons mezcal or good-quality
    tequila (optional)
½ tablespoon pure vanilla extract

MEZCAL

Mezcal is considered by many to be the mother of tequila. It was first produced from wild agave, or *maguey*, in Oaxaca. In my experience, there is nothing better than drinking warm, fresh mezcal right from the still on a dusty road near the archaeological ruins in Mitla, in a little village called Santiago Matalan, in Oaxaca. Mezcal's high alcoholic content and rumored hallucinogenic effects seem to have blocked any memory of the pungent smells of the burros that, to this day, pull the stone wheels that press the juice from the maguey.

JAMAICA LIMONADA
HIBISCUS FLOWER LEMONADE

A real summer cooler that, alternatively, can be made into a frozen treat by using half the water and blending the lemonade with a dozen ice cubes in an electric blender. This also makes a great margarita mixer. *Jamaica* is the Spanish word for dried hibiscus blossoms, which are found in almost every market in Central Mexico. They are used for *agua fresca*, which is similar to an iced tea, and for desserts and candies.

8 cups water
1 cup large dried hibiscus flowers
1 (6-ounce) can frozen lemonade
    concentrate
1 cup sugar
6 slices lemon, for garnish

Serves 6

In a medium-size pan, combine the water and hibiscus flowers and bring to a boil. Remove and let the flowers steep until the water is cool. Strain the liquid into the jar of an electric blender, add the lemonade and sugar, and blend. Pour into tall glasses, add a lemon slice to each glass for garnish, and serve.

CAFÉ DE OLLA

This sweet, strong coffee drink is another beloved morning-time beverage in Mexico. It's also a favorite for dipping *Conchas* (page 172). Some people add a few anise seeds or cloves to the mixture.

1 cup water
1 cup finely chopped piloncillo or firmly
    packed dark brown sugar
4 cups freshly brewed espresso or other
    strong, dark roast coffee
2 cinnamon sticks, preferably Mexican

Serves 8

In a saucepan, combine the water and *piloncillo,* and bring to a simmer. Remove from the heat and let sit until the sugar is dissolved.

Brew the coffee, add the cinnamon sticks and as much of the *piloncillo* syrup as desired to the pot, and serve hot.

ROMPOPE

This rich, creamy drink is similar to eggnog. It is a Christmas Eve or Christmas Day staple.

3 cups milk
3 cups heavy cream
1½ cups sugar
1 vanilla bean, split and scraped
Zest of 1 orange
½ teaspoon ground nutmeg
6 egg yolks
½ cup bottled light Caribbean spiced rum
½ cup orange liqueur (such as Grand
    Marnier) or brandy

Serves 6

In a heavy, medium-size pan, combine the milk, cream, ¾ cup of the sugar, the vanilla bean and seeds, the orange zest, and the nutmeg and bring just to a boil. Remove from the heat.

In a bowl, whisk the egg yolks with the remaining ¾ cup of sugar. Slowly pour about 1 cup of the hot milk into the egg yolks, beating constantly, to warm them. Return the egg mixture to the hot milk, beating continuously. Return the pan to low heat and cook until the mixture thickens and coats the back of a wooden spoon. When the mixture is thick, remove the pan from the heat, strain it into a clean bowl, and let it cool. After it has cooled, stir in the rum and liqueur. Pour into 6 glasses and serve chilled over ice.

SANGRITA

Mexicans are very devoted tequila drinkers. Many purists serve *Sangrita*, this spicy-sweet-salty tomato and citrus juice drink, and chase it with a shot of pure tequila on the side. The name means "little blood," which is not nearly as appealing as this refreshing libation is. Try it in a mixed drink, like a Bloody Maria—it's delicious.

Serves 8

Combine all of the ingredients except the tequila in a large pitcher and chill for at least 2 hours. Serve in tall glasses over crushed ice. Serve 1½-ounce shots of tequila separately.

2 cups tomato juice
1 cup freshly squeezed orange juice
½ cup freshly squeezed grapefruit juice
¼ cup freshly squeezed lime juice
¼ cup grenadine
2 tablespoons Maggi sauce or
   Worcestershire sauce
1 tablespoon hot sauce (such as Tabasco)
12 ounces silver tequila (see sidebar, page
   197), served on the side as shots

MICHELADA

More sophisticated than a beer with a squeeze of lime, a *michelada* will slake even the biggest thirst. Use dark or light Mexican beer, depending on your preference.

Serves 1

Run the cut side of the lime around the rim of a highball or pilsner glass and then dip in the salt. Fill the glass with ice. Squeeze in the lime, add the Tabasco and Maggi or Worcestershire sauce, and pour the beer over the ice.

½ lime
Coarse salt, for rimming the edge of the
   glass
2 dashes Tabasco sauce or your favorite
   brand of Mexican hot sauce
2 dashes Maggi sauce or Worcestershire
   sauce
1 (12-ounce) bottle Mexican beer

PALOMA

Another popular Mexican drink is a Paloma. Fill a tall glass with ice, pour in a shot of tequila (1½ ounces) and 1 tablespoon of freshly squeezed lime juice, add about half a can (½ cup) of Squirt or other grapefruit-flavored soda, stir, garnish with a lime slice, and serve.

DOS CAMINOS MARGARITA

Making *great* margaritas depends on far more than the tequila you choose to use. I think a fresh fruit base is the key to true margarita dominance. Also, even though margaritas are traditionally made with lime juice only, a little bit of lemon gives a nice bright lift to the taste. Be sure to really shake the cocktail shaker hard, because a good shake wakes up the cocktail and brings out all the spices of the tequila. Margaritas can be made separately or in a large shaker. The kosher salt to rim the glass is optional, although shaking up the cocktail with a tiny pinch of salt is also quite tasty. This recipe may easily be doubled and it can be made in an electric blender with crushed ice, if you prefer.

Makes 16 small margaritas

Fill a cocktail shaker with ice.

FOR EACH MARGARITA: Add the fruit mix along with the tequila and Triple Sec and a dash of salt. Shake hard 20 times.

To rim a glass with salt, pour about ¼ inch of salt into a small, flat dish. Run a lime wedge around the outside top of the glass. Invert the glass into the salt.

Pour over fresh ice or serve straight up.

BASIC FRUIT MIX

1 cup freshly squeezed lime juice

½ cup freshly squeezed lemon juice

½ cup Simple Syrup (page 187)

FOR EACH OF THE 16 SMALL MARGARITAS:

1 ounce fruit mix (above)

1½ ounces tequila

½ ounce Triple Sec

Kosher or coarse salt, to rim the glasses (optional)

1 lime, cut into wedges

TEQUILA

The three main types of tequila are *plata* or "silver" (also called *blanco* or "white"), which is bottled without being aged; *reposado,* meaning "rested," which is aged in oak for at least two months; and *añejo,* which is aged for at least a year. Recently, some distillers are making a super *añejo* that is aged over two years. These aged tequilas are wonderful for sipping like good cognac or whiskey.

CHIPOTLE BLOODY MARIA

While the Bloody Mary was actually invented in Paris, this Mexican twist on the classic version will wake up your taste buds in the morning or at any time of the day or evening. This recipe is easily doubled for a crowd.

4 cups V-8 or other tomato-based
    vegetable juice
2 tablespoons freshly squeezed lime juice
2 tablespoons prepared horseradish
1 tablespoon freshly ground black pepper
1 tablespoon Worcestershire sauce
1 tablespoon kosher salt
½ to 1 tablespoon celery salt
½ to 1 tablespoon garlic powder
½ tablespoon Tabasco sauce
1 canned chipotle chilies in adobo
2 cups silver tequila (such as El Tesoro
    Platinum or other light tequila)
8 ribs celery, for garnish
8 lime wedges, for garnish

Serves 8

Combine all of the ingredients except the tequila, the celery, and the lime wedges in the jar of an electric blender, and quickly blend to mix. Adjust seasonings to taste. Fill 8 (12-ounce) glasses about half full with ice. Add ¼ cup of tequila to each glass. Pour in ½ cup of the Bloody Maria mix, stir, garnish each glass with a rib of celery and a lime wedge, and serve.

BLOODY MARIA, STRAIGHT UP

To make a chilled Bloody Maria with no rocks: For each drink, put several ice cubes, ½ cup of the Bloody Maria mixture, and ¼ cup tequila into a martini shaker, and shake vigorously. Strain into a highball glass or martini glass, garnish with lime, and serve.

POMEGRANATE SANGRIA

Sangria is a great choice when you want your drinks to say "fiesta." Few are as exciting to serve as this fruity-spiced version. Many supermarkets now sell pomegranate juice. Each fresh pomegranate yields about one-half cup of juice. Dry red wine from the Rioja region of Spain is traditionally used in this drink. Be sure to allow the fruit to marinate for at least a couple hours, or preferably overnight.

Serves 6

JUICE TWO OF THE POMEGRANATES: Separate the seeds from the core. Put the seeds in a mesh strainer and press them with the back of a large kitchen spoon. You should have about 1 cup of juice.

Remove the seeds from the remaining pomegranate. Combine the seeds in a large pitcher or bowl with the orange, lemon, apple, pear, cloves, and cinnamon stick. Stir in the pomegranate juice, wine, cranberry juice, grenadine, and Cointreau. Refrigerate for at least two hours or overnight. Add ice and serve.

3 fresh pomegranates, or 1 cup pomegranate juice, plus 1 fresh pomegranate

1 large Navel orange, sliced

1 lemon, sliced

1 sweet apple (such as Golden Delicious), cored and diced

1 pear, cored and diced

2 whole cloves

1 stick cinnamon, prefreably Mexican

1 (750-milliliter) bottle dry red wine, such as Rioja from Spain

1 cup white cranberry juice

1 cup grenadine

1 cup Cointreau, Grand Marnier, or citrus brandy

WHITE SANGRIA
WITH FRESH STRAWBERRIES, MANGO, AND MINT

Spanish white wines, like Albariño or Rueda, work particularly well for this version of sangria. Sauvignon blanc and pinot grigio will also work. I believe the secret to really good sangria is a shot of Grand Marnier or other citrus brandy. I also include a can of lemon-lime soda to add a hint of carbonation.

1 bunch fresh mint

2 (750-millileter) bottles dry white wine
   (see headnote for suggestions)

1 large ripe mango, peeled and cubed (see
   sidebar, page 149)

1 pint fresh strawberries, hulled and sliced

1 Navel orange, sliced into rings

1 lemon, sliced into rings

½ cup orange liqueur (such as Grand
   Marnier) or brandy or rum

1 (12-ounce) can lemon-lime soda
   or club soda

Serves 6

Using the handle of a wooden spoon, bruise the mint to bring out its flavor, and then combine all of the ingredients except the ice in a large pitcher, refrigerate for at least 2 hours or overnight. Add plenty of ice and serve.

PONCHE

This traditional fruit punch definitely packs a "punch." Everyone has a personal favorite recipe—this is mine. In Mexico, and in my version, it starts with a frozen fruit punch concentrate, and then a bunch of different fresh fruits and fruit juices and any hard liquor that may be handy (usually tequila, rum, or mezcal) are thrown in. Be creative! When I was younger, we called this "Jungle Juice." We started with a large tin washtub, mixed the punch, fruit, juice, and ice, and then everyone brought a bottle of their favorite booze and dumped it in. Needless to say, I can't remember too many of these parties.

2 quarts fruit punch from concentrate
2 cups freshly squeezed orange juice
1 cup apple cider
2 cups diced watermelon or cantaloupe, or a
    combination of both
1 cup diced fresh pineapple
½ cup sliced strawberries
1 Navel orange, sliced crosswise into thin
    rings
2 lemons, sliced crosswise into thin rings
1 (12-ounce) bottle of grapefruit or lemon-
    lime soda
12 to 16 ounces silver tequila, rum, or
    brandy, or a combination of all three

Serves 8 or more

In a large punch bowl, prepare the punch according to the directions on the container. Stir in the orange juice and cider, add the fruits and soda, and add whichever alcoholic beverage you desire. Add ice and serve.

HOT SPICED CHAMOMILE CIDER

This holiday treat will cheer guests of all ages. For grownups, add a shot of rum or brandy to this festive hot beverage, if desired. You can also coat the rim of the cups with cinnamon and sugar by rubbing an apple wedge around the cup's rim and then dipping the rim into that sweet mixture. The cider may be made several hours in advance and reheated.

8 cups fresh apple cider
½ cup honey
4 allspice berries
2 cinnamon sticks, preferably Mexican, plus
    additional sticks for garnish
2 cloves
¼ cup chamomile flowers, or 4 chamomile
    tea bags
1 Granny Smith or other tart green apple,
    cored and cut into wedges, for garnish

Serves 8

In a medium-size saucepan, combine the cider, honey, allspice, cinnamon sticks, and cloves and bring to a simmer. Remove the pan from the heat, add the chamomile, and steep for 5 to 10 minutes, depending on how strong you like the flavor. Remove the cinnamon sticks and reserve. Pour the cider through a strainer. Ladle into cups, garnish each with a wedge of apple and a cinnamon stick, and serve.

GLOSSARY

Achiote: A seasoning paste made from ground annatto seeds, spices, and lime juice or vinegar.

Adobo: A smoky, chile-based marinade or seasoning with tomatoes, onions, garlic, and spices.

Al ajillo: A common Mexican preparation that combines the words for garlic—*ajo*—and *guajillo* chiles. These bright red chiles are very common throughout Mexico. They add a toasty, mild flavor, so the sauce is basically a decadently rich chile and garlic beurre blanc.

Albondigas: Mexican meatballs.

Al carbón: Any type of meat cooked over charcoal or wood coals.

Al pastor: "In the style of the shepherd." Any type of meat cooked over a spit, Middle Eastern style.

Annatto seeds: Small, round, bright red seeds that are ground and used in Yucatán's achiote paste.

Avocado leaves: The leaves harvested from Mexican avocado trees are sold fresh and dried in Mexican markets or online. In their dried form, they have a distinctive anise flavor and are used like a bay leaf in soups, sauces, and stocks. They are removed before serving.

Banana leaves: Used most frequently to wrap pork for *cochinita pibil* in the Yucatán, and for barbacoa in Oaxaca and tamales in other regions.

Barbacoa: A method of slowly cooking meat in an underground pit, usually wrapped in banana or agave leaves.

Cajeta: A specialty of Guanajuato and San Luis Potosí, in the north central part of Mexico, *cajeta* is *dulce de leche* made with goat's milk, or a combination of goat's and cow's milk, which is simmered with sugar and reduced to a thick consistency.

Canela/cinnamon sticks: The cinnamon used in Mexico comes from the loose-bark variety of the spice that is grown in Sri Lanka. Because it is softer, the sticks are easy to pulverize in a *molcajete* or an electric coffee grinder.

Carne asada: Grilled or broiled meat, usually skirt or flank steak, cooked quickly over hot coals.

Carnitas: A specialty, originally from Michoacán, a state on the western coast, in which cubes of pork are slowly simmered in fat and spices until meltingly tender and then used in tacos and burritos.

Ceviche: Raw or lightly cooked fish or shellfish marinated in citrus juice or other acid to cure, or "cook," them. In Mexico, the fish is traditionally mixed with tomatoes, onions, chiles, and spices, and the dish is served as an appetizer. Originally, this method was used to preserve raw fish before refrigeration was available.

Chayote: A smallish, pale green squash with smooth, slightly ridged skin. Although similar to zucchini, it has a firmer texture that requires longer cooking

Chiles, dried:

Ancho: A dried, ripe poblano pepper that is triangular in shape with a broad top that tapers to a blunt tip. The ancho is deep red with wrinkled, shiny skin and averages 4½ inches long and 3 inches across the top. Anchos have a fruity flavor with a slightly acidic bite. Most are mild, but some may be hot, depending on where they were grown, the soil, the climate, and the amount of water they receive. Similar in size and shape to mulato chiles, anchos can be distinguished by holding them up to a light. Anchos will have a reddish hue; mulatos will be chocolate brown.

Arbol: Ripened to bright red and then dried. As the name implies, the arbol grows on a bushy plant with woody stems. This smooth-skinned, slender chile tapers to a sharp point and measures about 3 inches long and ⅜ inch wide. It is thin-fleshed and very, very hot, with a sharp flavor that intensifies when lightly toasted. These chiles are most frequently used for hot table sauces, for frying whole and adding to dishes, like a pot of beans, or ground into a powder for a condiment for sliced fruit, cucumbers, or jicama.

Cascabel: A roundish, deep red-black chile with a smooth polished surface. As suggested by its name, when shaken, it makes a noise like a rattle. Available throughout Mexico, cascabels are widely used in the dishes of the central-western and northern parts of the country. Typically, it measures about 1¼ inches wide and 1 inch long. When rehydrated, the cascabel is quite fleshy and is pleasantly hot. It is most commonly used in table salsas.

Chipotle: A ripened jalapeño that is smoke-dried. There are two varieties: the large, tobacco brown *meco* and the mulberry-colored chipotle *mora* (or smaller *morita*). It is grown red and dries to a deep reddish-purple color. The average chipotle is 2½ inches long and 1 inch wide. It is very fleshy when rehydrated and very spicy. Highly versatile, chipotles are used for pickling and for flavoring soups, sauces, fish, and meat dishes. They are also available canned and packed in adobo sauce (see below).

Chipotle chiles in adobo sauce: Dried, smoked jalapeños typically canned in a thick tomato sauce that is seasoned with onions, garlic, and vinegar.

Guajillo: Literally meaning "big pod," this chile, along with the ancho, is the most commonly used in Mexico. Inexpensive and easy to come by, it is reddish in color, with a tough, shiny, smooth, opaque skin. The shape is an elongated triangle with narrow shoulders tapering to a pointed tip. On average, these chiles measure 1¼ inches across the top and about 5 inches long. They have a crisp, sharp flavor and can vary from very hot to hot. When rehydrated, the guajillo is fairly meaty, but the skin remains tough, so sauces made with this chile are usually strained. Guajillos are used for table sauces, enchiladas, adobos, and stews.

Mulato: Gets its name from its brown color. The mulato plant is essentially the same as the poblano, with slightly different genes that affect the color and taste of the fruit. When mature, the chiles are a very dark green and turn a rich brown as they ripen. Mulatos range from mild to fairly hot; they have a mild, sweetish taste that, along with their color, makes them especially suitable for *mole poblano*. When rehydrated, they are fleshy and have a mild, faintly chocolate taste.

Pasilla: The dried form of the chilaca chile. Also known as a *chile negro* in some parts of Mexico, the pasilla is a long, narrow chile with a blunt or slightly pointed end. The skin is very dark green to shiny black, and the surface is puckered with vertical ridges. An average-size pasilla chile is 6 inches long and 1 inch wide. It ranges from medium to fairly hot and, when rehydrated, it has a sharp but rich, earthy flavor. The chiles can be stuffed; used in table sauces, *moles*, and stews; fried whole; or cut into strips for a garnish.

Chiles, fresh:

Anaheim: Both the green and the red (ripened) stages of these mild chiles are used for stuffing, as in chiles rellenos, and can be diced or puréed. Although the outer skin is tough, once it is charred all over, it is easily removed. The red Anaheim is also called a Colorado chile. Mexican cooks like to dice or purée them and then add them to sauces, soups, and casseroles.

Chilaca: A long, narrow, dark green chile that often twists as it grows, the chilaca reaches up to 9 inches in length. As it ripens, the chile turns dark brown. It can be mild to medium hot, with a full flavor. When dried, it is known as a pasilla.

Habanero: Among the hottest of all chiles, this small, lantern-shaped pepper can be found in shades from light green to bright orange, when fully mature. The Mexican variety of this chile is grown in the Yucatán. Its uniquely fruity flavor is most often used as an accent in sauces. It is also used in its dry form.

Jalapeño: Smooth, dark-green-skinned chiles that turn bright red when ripe. Typically about 2 inches long with a somewhat rounded tip and up to 1 inch wide, they take their name from Jalapa, the capital of Veracruz. They range from hot to very hot, and they are readily available fresh in most markets. When dried and smoked, they are called chipotles. They are often available canned, packed in adobo sauce.

Poblano: Large, heart-shaped chiles with a rich, full flavor. Poblanos can be dark greenish-black to reddish-brown (and sweeter, richer tasting) when ripe. The chiles' thick walls make them good for stuffing, but often the skin is charred and removed before use. The dried chile is known as an ancho.

Scotch Bonnet: Among the hottest of all chile peppers, Scotch Bonnets resemble their close relative the habanero, but they are a little smaller. They range in color from yellow to orangy red.

Chorizo: Unlike the Spanish version of this sausage made with smoked meats and *pimentón de la vera* (smoked paprika), Mexican chorizo is made from fresh meat, ground red chiles, paprika, and sometimes achiote, making it reddish in color.

Dairy products:

Chihuahua: One of the most popular cow's milk cheeses in Mexico. Real Chihuahua is difficult to find, even in Mexico, because the Mennonite communities that produced it have since moved to Central America. It is high in butterfat and resembles young, mild Cheddar. When it is properly aged, Chihuahua can be quite tangy. High-quality domestic Muensters or medium Cheddars are good substitutes. Classic uses for this cheese include chiles rellenos, *queso fundido* (Mexican fondue), and quesadillas.

Crema: A soured milk product similar to crème fraîche or sour cream. Crema is a salty, white, drizzling cream that is thinner than sour cream and is used as a garnish or a dressing. Commercial sour cream thinned with a little milk or cream is a good substitute.

Queso Oaxaca: From the central valley of Oaxaca, this whole cow's milk string cheese is creamy in color and has a pleasant acidity to its bite. Typically sold as wound balls, it melts well and is used in various ways, from being shredded and used to top *bocaditos* to being used as a filling for quesadillas or chile rellenos. You can substitute mozzarella cheese.

Queso cotija: Named for the town in Michoacán in the west of Mexico where it was first made, *queso cotija* is a dry, aged cow's milk cheese that is prized for its salty bite. *Cotija* is not a good melting cheese, so it should be combined with another cheese in cooked dishes. It is perfect for crumbling and sprinkling on beans, soups, and salads, and it also stands alone for eating. Use it in the same manner as you would use grated Parmesan or Romano in cooking, or substitute feta or ricotta salata.

Queso fresco: A fresh cheese (as the name indicates) made with cow's milk that is produced all over Mexico. Other local names include *queso de metate, queso molido,* and *queso ranchero.* The cheese is used fresh, as a table cheese, crumbled as a topping, or as a stuffing for chiles or quesadillas because it melts well. It has a pleasant acidity and creaminess. It is similar to mild feta cheese, which will work in a pinch.

Enchilada: A corn tortilla rolled around a filling and topped with sauce and cheese.

Epazote: An herb with long, pointy, jagged leaves that tastes like a cross between mint, basil, and oregano. In a pinch, oregano may be used. Traditionally used in bean dishes (where it is said to reduce flatulence), and in egg and cheese dishes, epazote is best when young, with small leaves. As the leaves become mature, they develop a strong smell and an assertive taste.

Flauta: See **taquito.**

Hoja santa: An aromatic herb, also known as "sacred leaf," or "root beer plant." It smells somewhat like nutmeg or black pepper and is often used to season Mexican dishes, including *mole verde.* The taste is reminiscent of anise. The large leaf is sometimes used to wrap foods like tamales, fish, or poultry. If you cannot find *hoja santa,* substitute fresh tarragon leaves.

Huitlacoche/cuitlacoche: In Mexico, this corn fungus is a food delicacy to be savored. It is also called "Mexican truffle" or "Mexican caviar." The kernels have a smoky-sweet flavor.

Jicama: Also called "Mexican potato," this is a native root vegetable of Mexico and Central America. It looks like a large round potato, but it has a mild, sweet taste with a crunchy white interior that is similar in texture to an apple.

Lard: In Mexico, lard is used as the fat of choice for all types of frying, as well as in tamales and some types of tortilla products. While it has been relatively out of favor in the United States, recent studies show that it has less saturated fat than butter. In this book, we use lard but offer substitutes where applicable. But for certain dishes, lard adds a flavor that cannot be duplicated with any other fat, specifically in *mole* preparations, tamales, and *carnitas.* Lard is generally packaged like a pound of butter. When buying, check the "use by" date and make sure it is fresh. Lard must be refrigerated, or it can be frozen for several months if tightly wrapped.

Maggi sauce: Although this sauce is from China, it is sold in every Mexican supermarket and small food store. Maggi sauce tastes like a cross between Worcestershire and soy sauce, and it is used like Worcestershire sauce in marinades, soups, and anywhere a dash of salty seasoning is needed.

Mexican chocolate: A rustic chocolate, most famously from Oaxaca, that is flavored with cinnamon, almonds, and vanilla. The texture tends to be gritty or granular from the sugar. It is essential in dark *mole* sauce, where it gives richness without adding a cloyingly sweet aftertaste. The best-known brands are Ibarra and Abuelito.

Mexican oregano: Typically purchased dried or in flakes, this variety of oregano is somewhat stronger than its Greek, Italian, or Sicilian cousins and is slightly sweeter. It is widely used in Mexican cooking and is readily available on the Internet (see Sources).

Mojo de ajo: Toasted garlic sauce made with butter and lime juice. At Dos Caminos, we make many variations of basic *mojo de ajo* recipes by adding fruit, chiles, or tomatillos.

Moles: Complex sauces made with, but not exclusively, chiles, nuts, spices, fruits, vegetables, chocolate, and seasonings.

Nopales: Young pads from the prickly pear cactus. The needles are removed before cooking.

Piloncillo: Mexican raw sugar molded into flat-topped cones. *Piloncillo* can vary in taste from mildly caramel to a quite assertive, almost molasses flavor. Dark brown sugar is a good substitute.

Quesadilla: Fried or grilled flour or corn tortillas filled with cheese and/or other fillings.

Queso: See **dairy products.**

Quinoa: High-protein grain often used in salads or side dishes.

Salsa or table salsa: The essential condiment for many Mexican dishes. May be raw or cooked.

Sopes: Small, round cornmeal tartlets that are like thick tortillas with the edges pinched to form a ridge and then cooked on a griddle. *Sopes* can be made any size, and smaller ones are great as passed hors d'oeuvres.

Taco: Usually a fresh corn tortilla folded in half and filled with any combination of meat, cheese, vegetables, and condiments, including tomatoes, lettuce, and salsa.

Tamale: Coarse-ground corn *masa* dough filled with meat, vegetables, or fruit and wrapped in a corn husk and steamed.

Taquito: Both taquitos and flautas (which means flutes) are little tacos made of corn tortillas usually filled with meat, rolled up, and fried. Taquitos are smaller than flautas.

Tomatillo: A relative of the gooseberry family, the tomatillo resembles a small green tomato with a papery husk covering that is removed before using. Tomatillos slightly tart but very flavorful, and they are used in many sauces, especially green ones.

Torta: A Mexican-style sandwich on a roll that is cooked on a griddle.

Tortilla: A flat, thin, circular unleavened bread made from either corn flour or wheat flour. The most important item in Mexican cuisine.

Tostada: A crisp, flat fried corn tortilla. It is often topped with beans, meat, tomatoes, lettuce, and salsa.

Yerba buena: An herb in the mint family, popular in Mexican cooking. Substitute spearmint for this in cooking.

SOURCES

MAIL ORDER

Bueno Foods
2001 Fourth St. S.W.
Albuquerque, NM 87102
(505) 243-2722

Blazing Chile Bros.
(800) 473-9040

Calido Chile Traders
5360 Merriam Dr.
Merriam, KS 66203
(800) 568-8468

Caribbean Spice Company
2 S. Church St.
Fairhope, AL 36532
(800) 990-6088

Casados Farms
P.O. Box 1269
San Juan Pueblo, NM 87566
(505) 852-2433

Casa Lucas Market
2934 Twenty-fourth St.
San Francisco, CA 94110
(415) 826-4334

Central Market
4001 N. Lamar
Austin, TX 78756
(512) 306-1000

Chile Hill Emporium
328 San Felipe N.W.
Albuquerque, NM 87104
(505) 242-7538

Chili Patch, USA
204 San Felipe N.W.
Albuquerque, NM 87501
(800) 458-0646
(505) 242-4454

Chile Pepper Magazine
P.O. Box 80780
Albuquerque, NM 87198
(800) 359-1483
www.chilepeppermag.com

Chile Pepper Mania
1709-F Airline Highway
P.O. Box 232
Hollister, CA 95023
(408) 636-8259

The Chile Shop
109 East Water St.
Santa Fe, NM 87501
(505) 983-6080

Chile Today—Hot Tamale
919 Highway 33, Suite 47
Freehold, NJ 07728
(800) 468-7377
(908) 308-1151

Colorado Spice Company
5030 Nome St., Unit A
Denver, CO 80239
(303) 373-0141

Coyote Cocina
1364 Rufina Circle, No. 1
Santa Fe, NM 87501
(800) 866-HOWL

Dean and DeLuca
560 Broadway
New York, NY 10012
(212) 431-1691
www.dean-deluca.com

Don Alfonso Foods
P.O. Box 201988
Austin, TX 78720
(800) 456-6100

Enchanted Seeds
P.O. Box 6087
Las Cruces, NM 88006
(505) 233-3033

Flamingo Flats
P.O. Box 441
St. Michael's, MD 21663
(800) 421-9477

Frieda's, Inc.
P.O. Box 584888
Los Angeles, CA 90058
(800) 421-9477

GMB Specialty Foods, Inc.
P.O. Box 962
San Juan Capistrano, CA 92693-0962
(714) 240-3053

Hot-Hot-Hot
56 South Delacey Ave.
Old Town Pasadena, CA
(800) 959-7742
(818) 564-1090

Hot Sauce Club of America
P.O. Box 687
Indian Rocks Beach, FL 34635-0687
(800) SAUCE-2-U

Hot Sauce Harry's
The Dallas Farmer's Market
3422 Flair Dr.
Dallas, TX 75229
(214) 902-8552

Josie's
1130 Agua Fria
Santa Fe, NM 87501
(505) 983-6520

Kitchen Market
218 Eighth Ave.
New York, NY 10011
(212) 243-4433

La Palma Market
2884 Twenty-fourth St.
San Francisco, CA 94110
(415) 647-1500

Las Americas Grocery
235 West Valley Ave.
Homewood, AL 35209-3626
(205) 945-1639

Le Saucier, Inc.
1241 Hancock St.
Quincy, MA
(617) 227-9649

Melissa's World Variety Produce
P.O. Box 21127
Los Angeles, CA 90021
(800) 468-7111

Mercado Latino
148-C Common Dr.
El Paso, TX 79901
(915) 595-3195

Midwest Imports
1121 S. Clinton
Chicago, IL 60607
(312) 939-8400

Mi Rancho Market
464 Seventh St.
Oakland, CA 94607
(510) 451-2393

Mo Hotta, Mo Betta
P.O. Box 4136
San Luis Obispo, CA 93403
(800) 462-3220

Panchito's at the Market
Historic North Market
59 Spruce St.
Columbus, Ohio 43215
(614) 221-6394

Nancy's Specialty Market
P.O. Box 327
Wye Mills, MD 21679
(800) 462-6291

Old Southwest Trading Company
P.O. Box 7545
Albuquerque, NM 87194
(505) 836-0168

Pendery's
304 E. Belknap
Fort Worth, TX 76102
(800) 533-1870

Pepper Gal
P.O. Box 23006
Ft. Lauderdale, FL 33307
(305) 537-5540

Pepper Joe's, Inc.
7 Tyburn Court
Timonium, MD 21093
(410) 561-8158

Reyna Foods
2023 Penn Ave.
Pittsburgh, PA 15222
(412) 261-2606

Santa Fe School of Cooking
116 W. San Francisco St
Santa Fe, NM 87501
(505) 983-4511

Shepherd Garden Seeds
6116 Highway 9
Felton, CA 95018
(408) 335-6910

12th St. Cantina
1136 Arch St.
Philadelphia, PA 19107
(215) 625-0321

Williams-Sonoma
P.O. Box 7456
San Francisco, CA 94120
(415) 421-4555
www.williams-sonoma.com

INTERNET
www.amazon.com
www.americanspice.com
www.gourmetsleuth.com
www.inmamaskitchen.com
www.MexGrocer.com
www.rsmexfoods.com
www.salsasetc.com
www.texmextogo.com

METRIC CONVERSIONS AND EQUIVALENTS

OVEN TEMPERATURES

To convert Fahrenheit to Celsius, subtract 32 from Fahrenheit, multiply the result by 5, then divide by 9.

Description	Fahrenheit	Celsius	British Gas Mark
Very cool	200°	95°	0
Very cool	225°	110°	¼
Very cool	250°	120°	½
Cool	275°	135°	1
Cool	300°	150°	2
Warm	325°	165°	3
Moderate	350°	175°	4
Moderately hot	375°	190°	5
Fairly hot	400°	200°	6
Hot	425°	220°	7
Very hot	450°	230°	8
Very hot	475°	245°	9

COMMON INGREDIENTS AND THEIR APPROXIMATE EQUIVALENTS

1 cup uncooked rice = 225 grams

1 cup all-purpose flour = 140 grams

1 stick butter (4 ounces • ½ cup • 8 tablespoons) = 110 grams

1 cup butter (8 ounces • 2 sticks • 16 tablespoons) = 220 grams

1 cup brown sugar, firmly packed = 225 grams

1 cup granulated sugar = 200 grams

Information compiled from a variety of sources, including *Recipes into Type* by Joan Whitman and Dolores Simon (Newton, MA: Biscuit Books, 2000); *The New Food Lover's Companion* by Sharon Tyler Herbst (Hauppauge, NY: Barron's, 1995); and *Rosemary Brown's Big Kitchen Instruction Book* (Kansas City, MO: Andrews McMeel, 1998).

APPROXIMATE METRIC EQUIVALENTS

Volume

¼ teaspoon	1 milliliter
½ teaspoon	2.5 milliliters
½ teaspoon	4 milliliters
1 teaspoon	5 milliliters
1¼ teaspoon	6 milliliters
1½ teaspoon	7.5 milliliters
1¾ teaspoon	8.5 milliliters
2 teaspoons	10 milliliters
1 tablespoon (½ fluid ounce)	15 milliliters
2 tablespoons (1 fluid ounce)	30 milliliters
¼ cup	60 milliliters
⅓ cup	80 milliliters
½ cup (4 fluid ounces)	120 milliliters
⅔ cup	160 milliliters
½ cup	180 milliliters
1 cup (8 fluid ounces)	240 milliliters
1¼ cups	300 milliliters
1½ cups (12 fluid ounces)	360 milliliters
1⅔ cups	400 milliliters
2 cups (1 pint)	460 milliliters
3 cups	700 milliliters
4 cups (1 quart)	0.95 liter
1 quart plus ¼ cup	1 liter
4 quarts (1 gallon)	3.8 liters

Weight

¼ ounce	7 grams
½ ounce	14 grams
½ ounce	21 grams
1 ounce	28 grams
1¼ ounces	35 grams
1½ ounces	42.5 grams
1⅔ ounces	45 grams
2 ounces	57 grams
3 ounces	85 grams
4 ounces (¼ pound)	113 grams
5 ounces	142 grams
6 ounces	170 grams
7 ounces	198 grams
8 ounces (½ pound)	227 grams
16 ounces (1 pound)	454 grams
35.25 ounces (2.2 pounds)	1 kilogram

Length

⅛ inch	3 millimeters
¼ inch	6 millimeters
½ inch	1¼ centimeters
1 inch	2½ centimeters
2 inches	5 centimeters
2½ inches	6 centimeters
4 inches	10 centimeters
5 inches	13 centimeters
6 inches	15¼ centimeters
12 inches (1 foot)	30 centimeters

METRIC CONVERSION FORMULAS

To Convert	Multiply
Ounces to grams	Ounces by 28.35
Pounds to kilograms	Pounds by .454
Teaspoons to milliliters	Teaspoons by 4.93
Tablespoons to milliliters	Tablespoons by 14.79
Fluid ounces to milliliters	Fluid ounces by 29.57
Cups to milliliters	Cups by 236.59
Cups to liters	Cups by .236
Pints to liters	Pints by .473
Quarts to liters	Quarts by .946
Gallons to liters	Gallons by 3.785
Inches to centimeters	Inches by 2.54

INDEX